No Experience? No Problem!
Investing in Stocks with AI Assistance

Learn How to Use AI to Make
Smart Investment Choices from Day One

Ernie Braveboy

Copyright © 2024 by Ernie Braveboy

All rights reserved. No part of this publication may be reproduced, distributed, or transmitted in any form or by any means, including photocopying, recording, or other electronic or mechanical methods, without the prior written permission of the publisher, except in the case of brief quotations embodied in critical reviews and certain other noncommercial uses permitted by copyright law.

Table of Contents

Preface 1
    Acknowledgments.. 2
    How to Use This Book... 3

01: Introduction to Investing... 6
    What is Investing?... 8
    Why Invest in Stocks and ETFs?.. 10
    Common Investment Terminology................................... 13

02: The Basics of Stocks and ETFs.................................... 16
    Understanding Stocks: The Building Blocks of the Stock Market... 19
    What are ETFs and How Do They Work?........................ 21

03: First Steps in the Stock Market.................................. 27
    Setting Up Your Investment Account............................... 30
    How to Buy Your First Stock... 32
    Essential Tips for New Investors....................................... 35

04: Introduction to Artificial Intelligence in Investing... 38
    What is Artificial Intelligence?... 41
    How AI is Transforming Investing.................................... 43
    Benefits of AI for Individual Investors............................. 45

05: AI Tools and Platforms for Investors......................... 48
    Overview of Popular AI Investment Tools...................... 51
    How to Use Robo-Advisors.. 53
    AI-Powered Stock Analysis and Prediction Tools........... 56

06: Making Smart Investment Choices with AI 59

How AI Can Help You Choose Stocks 61

Integrating AI into Your Investment Strategy.......................64

Case Studies: AI Success Stories 66

07: Managing Your Investment Portfolio 70

Portfolio Management Basics 73

How AI Can Optimize Your Portfolio...................................75

When to Buy and Sell: AI Insights 78

08: Advanced AI Investing Techniques 81

Algorithmic Trading 84

Machine Learning Models for Predicting Stock Performance 87

Advanced AI Tools for Risk Assessment...............................90

09: The Future of Investing with AI 93

Emerging Trends in AI and Investing 95

How to Stay Updated with AI Investment Technologies....................98

Preparing for the Future of the Stock Market......................100

10: Building a Long-Term Investment Plan 104

Long-Term Investment Strategies.......................................107

Incorporating AI into Long-Term Planning........................110

Sustaining Growth: AI and Continuous Learning 112

Glossary of Investment and AI Terms 115

Appendix A: How to Access and Use Investment Platforms..........119

Appendix B: Resources for Further Learning 122

Index..124

About the Author 128

PREFACE

Welcome to "No Experience? No Problem! Investing in Stocks with AI Assistance: Learn How to Use AI to Make Smart Investment Choices from Day One." This book is designed with one goal in mind: to make the seemingly complex world of stocks and ETFs accessible to everyone, especially those who have never invested before. The use of Artificial Intelligence (AI) in investing can seem daunting, but this book will show you how AI can simplify and enhance the investment process.

Investing is not just for the wealthy or the experienced. It is a skill that anyone can learn and master with the right tools and knowledge. That's where AI comes into play. AI technologies have revolutionized many aspects of our lives, and investing is no exception. They offer new ways to analyze data, predict market trends, and make informed decisions quickly and efficiently—capabilities that were once available only to professional traders in large financial institutions.

Throughout this book, you will find a step-by-step guide to understanding the stock market, choosing your first investments, and using AI to assist and refine your investment strategy. Each chapter is crafted to build your knowledge from the ground up, ensuring that by the end, you will not only understand the basic principles of investing but also how to leverage the latest AI tools to your advantage.

I have also included real-life examples, case studies, and practical advice to help you apply what you've learned. My hope is that this book will not only educate you but also inspire confidence to actively participate in the financial markets.

Whether you are a student, a professional, or someone simply curious about investing, this book is for you. Let's demystify the world of financial investment together, and may this journey bring you both knowledge and financial growth.

Thank you for choosing this book to begin your investment journey. I am excited to help you unlock the potential of AI-assisted investing.

Ernie Braveboy

Acknowledgments

Writing this book has been an enlightening journey, one that would not have been possible without the support and encouragement of many individuals.

First and foremost, I would like to express my deepest gratitude to my family for their unwavering support and patience throughout the process of researching and writing this book. Their belief in my vision has been a constant source of strength.

I am immensely thankful to my colleagues and mentors in the fields of finance and technology, whose insights and expertise have been invaluable. Their willingness to share knowledge and offer critical feedback has enriched the content of this book immeasurably.

A special thanks goes to the team at Braveboy Publications. Their dedication and professionalism turned the manuscript into a polished final product. I am particularly grateful to my editor, Jane Doe, whose keen eye and thoughtful suggestions have greatly enhanced the clarity and flow of the text.

I must also acknowledge the vibrant community of AI developers and financial analysts whose innovative work continues to inspire and challenge investors around the world. The tools and case studies discussed in this book are a testament to their pioneering efforts.

Lastly, I extend my appreciation to you, the readers, who are embarking on your own investing journeys. This book was written for you, and I hope it serves as a valuable guide as you navigate the exciting world of AI-assisted investing.

Thank you all for making this book possible.

Ernie Braveboy

How to Use This Book

This book is structured to take you step-by-step through the basics of investing, all the way to utilizing advanced AI tools to enhance your financial decisions. Whether you are a complete beginner or someone with a bit of background knowledge, this guide aims to equip you with a solid understanding and practical skills to start investing confidently.

1. Sequential Reading:

For the best learning experience, I recommend reading this book from start to finish. Each chapter builds on the information provided in the previous ones, starting with fundamental concepts and gradually introducing more complex ideas and strategies.

2. Focus on Key Concepts:

Each chapter contains key concepts highlighted in boxes or bolded text. These are crucial for understanding the broader topics discussed and will be pivotal when you start applying what you've learned.

3. Practical Exercises:

At the end of each chapter, there are practical exercises designed to help you apply the concepts to real-world scenarios. These exercises will encourage you to engage with the material actively and start thinking like an investor.

4. Use of Case Studies:

Throughout the book, you will find case studies illustrating how real investors use AI to make decisions. Analyze these carefully to understand not just the "how" but also the "why" behind their strategies.

5. Glossary and Appendices:

Refer to the glossary for definitions of investment terms that are new or unfamiliar. The appendices provide additional resources, such as how to access and use specific AI investment tools, which can be especially useful as you begin to explore investing on your own.

6. Continuous Reference:

Keep this book handy as a reference guide. As you grow more comfortable and gain experience, you will find different sections more relevant. Revisiting chapters as you progress in your investing journey can provide new insights and reinforce your learning.

7. Interactive Components:

Where available, use the links and interactive components included in the digital version of this book. These can provide up-to-date information and additional learning opportunities.

By following these guidelines, you will maximize your learning experience with "No Experience? No Problem! Investing in Stocks with

AI Assistance." This book isn't just a read; it's a tool to launch and support your journey in the world of investing.

01
INTRODUCTION TO INVESTING

What iPs Investing?

Investing is the act of allocating resources, usually money, with the expectation of generating an income or profit. You can invest in endeavors, such as using money to start a business, or in assets, such as purchasing real estate in hopes of reselling it later at a higher price. However, in this book, we will focus primarily on investing in the stock market, which includes stocks, bonds, ETFs (Exchange Traded Funds), and other securities.

Why Invest?

The primary goal of investing is to make your money work for you. While saving money is crucial for financial security, investing allows you to grow your wealth significantly over time, often outpacing inflation and increasing your purchasing power. Furthermore, investing can provide you with additional income streams, help fund your retirement, or even get you out of a financial pinch, assuming adequate returns.

The Importance of Investing Early

Starting your investment journey early can significantly impact the total growth of your investments due to the power of compound interest. This is where your earnings on an investment generate their own earnings, which compounds over time. The earlier you start, the more benefit you gain from compounding.

Understanding Risk

All investments come with a level of risk. Generally, the higher the potential return, the higher the risk of loss. Understanding your personal risk tolerance—how much risk you can afford to take without undue stress—is crucial in choosing the right investments.

Investment Vehicles

There are several types of investment vehicles:

- **Stocks:** Shares of ownership in a company.
- **Bonds:** Loans made to a company or government (corporate or government bonds).
- **Mutual Funds:** Pooled money from many investors used to buy a diversified portfolio of stocks and bonds.
- **ETFs:** Similar to mutual funds, but traded on stock exchanges like individual stocks.
- **Real Estate:** Physical land or property.

Basic Strategies for Beginners

- **Diversification:** Don't put all your eggs in one basket. Spread your investments across different types of assets to mitigate risk.
- **Consistent Investing:** Consider regular investments to reduce the impact of price volatility.

- **Long-term Perspective:** Investing is most effective as a long-term endeavor. Patience can be more rewarding than trying to time the market.

Chapter Summary

Investing is a powerful tool for growing wealth and achieving financial independence. By understanding the basics and starting early, you can take advantage of compounding returns and mitigate risks through informed strategies. The next chapters will delve deeper into the specifics of stock market investing and how AI can help streamline and enhance your investment decisions.

What is Investing?

Investing is the act of committing resources, typically money, to an asset or endeavor with the expectation of earning a profit or generating income. It involves purchasing assets with the aim of having them increase in value over time. When you invest, you are essentially putting your money into vehicles that might earn more money for you in the future.

Key Concepts in Investing

- **Return on Investment (ROI):** This is the gain or loss on an investment relative to the amount of money invested. It is usually expressed as a percentage.
- **Assets:** These are resources with economic value that an individual, corporation, or country owns or controls with the expectation that it will provide future benefits. Assets include stocks, bonds, real estate, precious metals, and more.

- **Capital Appreciation:** This is an increase in the price or value of assets. It is one of the primary goals of investing.

- **Income Investment:** This refers to investments that provide regular income, such as dividends from stocks or interest from bonds.

- **Risks and Returns:** Generally, higher risks are associated with higher potential returns. The risk is that the actual return may vary and can result in potential losses.

- **Liquidity:** This refers to how easily an investment can be converted into cash without significantly affecting its value.

Types of Investments

- **Stocks:** When you buy shares of a company, you are buying a portion of that company. Stocks are popular investment vehicles because they can offer impressive growth (capital appreciation) and dividends.

- **Bonds:** Investing in bonds means loaning your money to an entity (a corporation or government) in exchange for periodic interest payments plus the return of the bond's face value when it matures. Bonds are typically considered safer than stocks.

- **Mutual Funds:** These pool money from many investors to purchase a diversified portfolio of stocks and/or bonds. Mutual funds are managed by financial professionals.

- **Real Estate:** Purchasing property as an investment involves more significant initial capital and can include rental properties or buying to sell at a higher price later.

- **ETFs (Exchange-Traded Funds):** Similar to mutual funds but traded on stock exchanges. ETFs hold assets like stocks, commodities, or bonds and generally operate with an arbitrage mechanism designed to keep trading close to its net asset value, though deviations can occasionally occur.

Why Invest?

The primary purpose of investing is not just to preserve your money but to grow it. Whether for retirement, the education of children, or generating wealth, investing is essential to achieving financial goals and increasing financial security. The power of compound interest, where your earnings generate more earnings over time, underscores the importance of starting to invest early and responsibly managing your investments to maximize returns.

Why Invest in Stocks and ETFs?

Investing in stocks and ETFs (Exchange-Traded Funds) offers several compelling benefits for investors, from the potential for significant returns to the ease of diversification. Here's a breakdown of why these investment vehicles are popular choices:

Potential for Growth

- **Stocks:** Historically, stocks have offered substantial return potential over the long term. By investing in stocks, you are buying a share of a company's future earnings and growth. As the company grows and becomes more valuable, so does your investment.

- **ETFs:** These funds often track a particular index, sector, commodity, or other assets but can be bought and sold like stocks. ETFs combine the potential for growth based on the underlying assets they represent, which can include a broad market index or specific sectors likely to experience growth.

Diversification

- **Reducing Risk:** Both stocks and ETFs provide opportunities for diversification. By spreading your investments across various stocks or purchasing ETFs that cover a wide range of sectors or geographical locations, you can reduce the impact of poor performance in any single investment.

- **ETFs and Instant Diversification:** One of the primary advantages of ETFs is that they offer instant diversification within a single investment. For example, an ETF that tracks the S&P 500 gives you exposure to 500 different large-cap U.S. companies across various industries.

Liquidity

- **Easy to Buy and Sell:** Stocks and ETFs are liquid assets, meaning they can be quickly and easily bought and sold during market hours. This liquidity is beneficial for investors who might need to convert their investments into cash quickly.

- **Transparency and Flexibility:** ETFs are particularly noted for their trading flexibility—they can be bought and sold at current market prices throughout the trading day, unlike mutual funds, which only trade at the end of the market day.

Income through Dividends

- **Income Generation:** Many stocks pay dividends, which can provide a regular income stream. These dividends can be reinvested or used as a source of regular income, depending on the investor's financial goals.

- **ETFs with Dividends:** Similarly, many ETFs pay out dividends accrued from the stocks within the fund. This can also enhance the compounding effect when dividends are reinvested.

Tax Efficiency

- **ETFs Are Generally More Tax-Efficient:** Compared to mutual funds, ETFs are often more tax-efficient due to their unique structure and the way transactions are executed. This can be beneficial for investors looking to minimize their tax liability on investment gains.

Accessibility

- **Wide Range of Choices:** The stock market offers a vast array of choices, from high-growth tech stocks to established dividend-paying companies. ETFs also cover a broad spectrum, from broad-market funds to niche sectors or strategies, providing options for all types of investors.

- **Low Entry Cost:** Many brokerage firms offer fractional shares of stocks and ETFs, allowing investors to start investing with small amounts of money. This makes it easier for individuals to build diversified portfolios, even with limited initial capital.

Investing in stocks and ETFs is an excellent way for individuals to participate in the financial markets and work towards their long-term financial objectives. Whether you're looking for growth, income, diversification, or all of the above, stocks and ETFs can play a pivotal role in your investment strategy.

Common Investment Terminology

Investing comes with its own language, and understanding these terms is essential for anyone looking to enter the stock market or manage their investments effectively. Below is a list of common investment terms that will help you navigate your investing journey with more confidence and insight.

Asset

Asset refers to any resource with economic value that an individual, corporation, or country owns or controls with the expectation that it will provide future benefit.

Bond

A **bond** is a fixed income instrument that represents a loan made by an investor to a borrower (typically corporate or governmental). Bonds are used by companies, municipalities, states, and sovereign governments to finance projects and operations.

Capital Gain

Capital Gain is the increase in the value of an investment or real estate that gives it a higher worth than the purchase price. The gain is not realized until the asset is sold.

Dividend

A **dividend** is a share of profits and retained earnings that a company pays out to its shareholders. When a corporation earns a profit or surplus, that money can be put to two uses: it can either be re-invested in the business or paid to shareholders as a dividend.

ETF (Exchange-Traded Fund)

An **ETF** is an investment fund traded on stock exchanges, much like stocks. An ETF holds assets such as stocks, commodities, or bonds and generally operates with an arbitrage mechanism designed to keep it trading close to its net asset value.

Liquidity

Liquidity refers to the ease with which an asset or security can be converted into ready cash without affecting its market price.

Market Volatility

Market Volatility refers to the rate at which the price of securities increases or decreases for a given set of returns. High volatility means that a security's price can change dramatically over a short time period in either direction.

Mutual Fund

A **mutual fund** is an investment program funded by shareholders that trades in diversified holdings and is professionally managed.

Portfolio

A **portfolio** is a collection of financial investments like stocks, bonds, commodities, and cash equivalents, along with their fund counterparts including mutual funds, exchange-traded funds, and closed funds.

Risk

Risk is the potential for losing some or all of the original investment. Different investments carry different levels of risk; investing in stocks is generally considered riskier than investing in government bonds.

Stock

A **stock** is a type of security that signifies ownership in a corporation and represents a claim on part of the corporation's assets and earnings.

Yield

Yield refers to the earnings generated and realized on an investment over a particular period of time. It is expressed as a percentage based on the invested amount, current market value, or face value of the security.

Understanding these terms will empower you to make informed decisions and effectively manage your investments. Whether you're discussing strategies with an advisor or researching potential investments on your own, this glossary will serve as a valuable resource.

02
THE BASICS OF STOCKS AND ETFS

In this chapter, we delve into the fundamental concepts of stocks and ETFs (Exchange-Traded Funds), two of the most popular investment vehicles. Understanding these basics is crucial for any investor looking to navigate the stock market successfully.

What are Stocks?

Stocks, also known as shares or equities, represent ownership in a company. When you buy stocks, you are essentially buying a piece of the company. If the company grows and becomes more valuable, so does your investment. Conversely, if the company suffers losses, the value of your investment can decrease.

Benefits of Investing in Stocks:

- **Potential for High Returns:** Historically, stocks have offered higher returns compared to many other types of investments over the long term.
- **Dividend Income:** Some stocks provide regular dividends, which are portions of the company's profit paid to shareholders.
- **Liquidity:** Stocks are highly liquid, meaning they can be quickly and easily sold in the stock market.

- **Ownership Rights:** Owning stocks means you get certain rights such as voting rights at shareholders' meetings and the ability to influence company decisions to some extent.

What are ETFs?

ETFs (Exchange-Traded Funds) are investment funds that are traded on stock exchanges, much like individual stocks. An ETF holds assets such as stocks, commodities, or bonds and generally operates with an arbitrage mechanism designed to keep its trading close to its net asset value, though deviations can sometimes occur.

Benefits of Investing in ETFs:

- **Diversification:** By owning an ETF, you gain exposure to a basket of securities, thereby spreading out risk.
- **Lower Costs:** Generally, ETFs have lower fees than mutual funds, making them an economical choice for individual investors.
- **Flexibility:** ETFs can be bought and sold at market price at any time during the trading day, providing greater flexibility than mutual funds.
- **Tax Efficiency:** ETFs are usually more tax-efficient than mutual funds due to their unique structure and how transactions are handled.

Comparing Stocks and ETFs

While both stocks and ETFs are essential components of many investment portfolios, they serve different purposes and carry different levels of risk.

- **Control vs. Diversification:** Buying individual stocks allows for more control over which companies you invest in, while ETFs offer instant diversification.

- **Risk Management:** Investing in a single stock is riskier than investing in an ETF that includes a diversified portfolio of stocks, as the impact of poor performance by a single company is lessened.

- **Cost Considerations:** Owning multiple individual stocks requires significant capital, whereas ETFs allow for diversified investments with much lower capital outlay.

How to Choose Between Stocks and ETFs?

The decision to invest in stocks or ETFs should be based on your investment goals, risk tolerance, and financial situation. Consider the following:

- **Investment Goals:** Are you looking for growth, income, or both? Your goals will influence whether you should invest in high-growth stocks, income-generating stocks, or diversified ETFs.

- **Risk Tolerance:** How much risk are you willing to accept? If you prefer a more conservative approach, ETFs might be more suitable due to their inherent diversification.

- **Time Horizon:** The length of time you plan to invest can also influence your decision. Long-term investors might lean towards ETFs for their compounding and less volatile nature.

In summary, stocks and ETFs both offer valuable opportunities for investors, but they come with different sets of features and risks. Understanding these can help you make informed decisions and build a portfolio that aligns with your financial objectives.

Certainly! Here's a section that explains the basics of stocks, titled "Understanding Stocks: The Building Blocks of the Stock Market," suitable for inclusion in your book "No Experience? No Problem! Investing in Stocks with AI Assistance":

Understanding Stocks: The Building Blocks of the Stock Market

Stocks, also known as equities, are fundamental units of ownership in public companies. When you buy a stock, you are purchasing a small piece of that company, making you a shareholder. Stocks are critical components of the financial world and serve as the primary means through which companies raise capital to grow, innovate, and expand their operations.

How Stocks Work

When a company decides to go public, it issues stocks through an Initial Public Offering (IPO). This process involves selling shares of the company to the public in exchange for cash. Once issued, these shares can be bought and sold among investors on various stock exchanges, like the New York Stock Exchange (NYSE) or the NASDAQ.

Types of Stocks

- **Common Stocks:** These are the most prevalent type of stocks that investors buy. Holders of common stocks typically have voting rights at shareholders' meetings (one vote per share) and receive dividends, which are a portion of the company's profits distributed to shareholders.

- **Preferred Stocks:** Unlike common stocks, preferred stocks generally do not provide voting rights. However, they offer a higher claim on assets and earnings than common stocks, which means dividends paid out to preferred shareholders are typically higher and more regular.

Why Companies Issue Stocks

- **Raising Capital**: Issuing stocks is a way for companies to raise money without incurring debt. This capital is then used for various purposes like expanding business operations, funding research and development, or paying off existing debts.

- **Liquidity and Valuation**: For company founders and early investors, selling stocks in a public offering provides an excellent opportunity to gain liquidity—converting shares into cash. Furthermore, trading on public markets establishes a clear market value for a company.

Benefits of Investing in Stocks

- **Potential for High Returns**: Historically, stocks have yielded higher returns than many other investment options, such as bonds or savings accounts, especially over long periods.

- **Ownership and Voting Rights**: Shareholders are part-owners of the company and can influence its direction through their voting rights.

- **Dividends**: Many companies pay regular dividends to their shareholders from their profits, providing an income stream in addition to potential capital gains.

Risks of Investing in Stocks

- **Market Risk**: Stock prices are subject to market fluctuations, influenced by factors like economic changes, political events, or company performance. This volatility can result in significant gains or losses.

- **Liquidity Risk**: While most stocks are highly liquid, some stocks, especially those of smaller companies, might be harder to sell quickly at a fair price.

- **No Guarantee of Dividends**: Not all stocks pay dividends, and even for those that do, the dividends can be cut if the company decides it needs to reinvest the profits or faces financial difficulties.

How to Start Investing in Stocks

For beginners, investing in stocks can seem daunting due to the risks involved. However, starting with a clear understanding of your financial goals, risk tolerance, and investing with a long-term perspective can mitigate these risks. It's also wise to diversify your stock investments by holding shares in various companies across different sectors.

Investors can buy stocks directly through a brokerage account or indirectly through mutual funds or ETFs that invest in a broad portfolio of stocks. This can provide the necessary diversification to protect against volatility and enhance potential returns.

What are ETFs and How Do They Work?

ETFs (Exchange-Traded Funds) are one of the most popular investment vehicles today, known for their versatility and cost-effectiveness. An ETF is a type of fund that owns underlying assets (like stocks, bonds, commodities, or real estate) and divides ownership of those assets into shares. ETF shares are bought and sold on public stock exchanges similar to ordinary stocks, which makes them highly accessible to investors.

Structure of ETFs

ETFs are structured to track an index, commodity, bonds, or a basket of assets like an index fund, but they trade like a stock on an exchange. This means they experience price changes throughout the day as they are bought and sold. ETFs typically have higher daily liquidity and lower fees than mutual fund shares, making them an attractive alternative for individual investors.

How ETFs Operate

- **Creation**: Initially, an ETF is created by a sponsor—the fund manager or financial institution—by assembling the underlying assets. The sponsor then forms shares that represent a claim on these assets.

- **Trading**: These shares are traded on stock exchanges, similar to stocks. This means investors can buy and sell ETF shares throughout the trading day at market price, which can fluctuate depending on the underlying assets' performance and market conditions.

- **Arbitrage Mechanism**: An ETF's price is kept in line with its underlying assets through an arbitrage mechanism. If an ETF's market price deviates from its net asset value (NAV), authorized participants (typically large financial institutions) will buy or sell ETF shares in large blocks, called creation units, to capitalize on the price difference and bring the ETF's market price back to its NAV.

Benefits of Investing in ETFs

- **Diversification**: Each ETF holds a portfolio of different assets, so with a single transaction, you can invest in a broad swath of the market. This spreads out risk, which can protect your investment from the volatility of individual assets.

- **Cost-Effective**: ETFs generally have lower management fees than actively managed mutual funds, and there are no sales loads. Also, because they are traded like stocks, investors can execute the same types of trades that they can with a stock, such as limit orders or short selling.

- **Tax Efficiency**: ETFs are more tax-efficient than mutual funds due to the way transactions are structured. Instead of redeeming shares for cash like mutual funds, ETFs are usually redeemed by exchanging securities, which minimizes taxable capital gains.

- **Transparency**: Most ETFs regularly disclose their holdings, offering transparency that allows investors to understand exactly what assets they are invested in and make informed decisions based on current market conditions.

Types of ETFs

- **Market ETFs**: Designed to track a particular index like the S&P 500 or NASDAQ.

- **Bond ETFs**: Invest in various types of bonds.

- **Sector and Industry ETFs**: Target specific industries or sectors of the economy.

- **Commodity ETFs**: Invest in commodities, such as gold or oil.

- **Style ETFs**: Track stocks that exhibit specific investment styles, such as large-cap, mid-cap, small-cap, growth, or value.

How to Invest in ETFs

Investing in ETFs involves setting up a brokerage account, after which you can buy and sell ETF shares as you would buy individual stocks. The flexibility to trade ETFs throughout the day allows investors to respond quickly to changes in the market or economic conditions.

Comparing Stocks and ETFs

Stocks and ETFs are both popular investment options, but they cater to different investment strategies and preferences. Understanding their distinctions can help you decide which is better suited to your investment goals and risk tolerance.

Ownership and Control

- **Stocks:** When you buy stocks, you are purchasing shares of a single company. This makes you a shareholder with ownership in that company, which might include voting rights and a direct stake in the company's profits and losses.

- **ETFs:** Buying an ETF means investing in a fund that holds assets such as stocks, bonds, or commodities from different entities. While you benefit from the diversified holdings, you do not own shares in the underlying companies directly and usually have no voting rights associated with these holdings.

Diversification

- **Stocks:** Investing in individual stocks can offer high returns if the stock performs well, but it also exposes you to higher risk if the company underperforms. The lack of diversification can make your investment more volatile.

- **ETFs:** ETFs inherently provide diversification within the asset classes they track. By owning an ETF, you reduce the risk of significant losses from the underperformance of any single stock or asset, as the risk is spread across different holdings.

Transaction Costs and Management Fees

- **Stocks:** Transaction costs for stocks typically include brokerage fees each time you buy or sell shares. There are no ongoing management fees for holding individual stocks.

- **ETFs:** Like stocks, buying and selling ETFs incurs brokerage fees, but ETFs also come with management fees, although these are generally lower than those of mutual funds. These fees are part of the expense ratio, which can affect the overall return on investment.

Trading and Pricing

- **Stocks:** Stocks are priced and can be traded throughout the trading day based on market supply and demand. Prices can fluctuate significantly during the day based on news, economic events, and market trends.

- **ETFs:** ETFs also trade throughout the day at market prices that can vary. However, an ETF's price is tied to the underlying net asset value of the holdings, which helps stabilize price movements compared to individual stocks.

Income Generation

- **Stocks:** Many stocks pay dividends, which provide shareholders with a share of the company's profits on a regular basis.

- **ETFs:** ETFs that hold dividend-paying stocks or interest-generating bonds also distribute these earnings to their shareholders. The income from an ETF depends on the performance of its entire portfolio.

Suitability for Investors

- **Stocks:** Stocks are well-suited for investors who wish to actively manage their portfolios and are comfortable with researching and selecting individual companies. They are suitable for those with higher risk tolerance aiming for specific high-growth opportunities.

- **ETFs:** ETFs are ideal for investors seeking a more passive investment approach, allowing them to gain broad market exposure or specific sector exposure without the need to analyze individual stocks. They are also well-suited for new investors or those with lower risk tolerance.

Conclusion

Choosing between stocks and ETFs depends largely on your investment strategy, risk tolerance, and the level of involvement you want in managing your investments. Stocks offer the potential for high returns and direct ownership, while ETFs provide an easy way to achieve diversification and reduce risk. Both can be integral parts of a balanced investment portfolio, and many investors choose to include both stocks and ETFs to capitalize on their unique benefits.

03
FIRST STEPS IN THE STOCK MARKET

Venturing into the stock market can be exciting and daunting in equal measure. This chapter will guide you through the initial steps necessary to begin your investment journey with confidence and clarity.

Understanding the Market

Before investing, it's crucial to understand how the stock market works. The market is a complex system where shares of publicly traded companies are issued and traded. It's influenced by various factors including economic indicators, corporate performance, political events, and market sentiment.

Setting Up Your Investment Account

- **Choose a Brokerage**: The first step is to select a brokerage firm. Brokerages act as the middleman between buyers and sellers in the stock market. You can choose from traditional brokerages, online brokerages, or robo-advisors depending on your investment style and needs.
- **Opening an Account**: Once you've chosen a brokerage, you'll need to open an investment account. This process typically involves providing personal information, setting up funding

options, and choosing the type of account (e.g., individual, joint, retirement).

- **Understanding Account Types**: It's important to understand the differences between taxable accounts and tax-advantaged accounts like IRAs or 401(k)s, as these can affect your investment decisions and tax obligations.

Basic Investment Principles

- **Risk Assessment**: Understanding your own risk tolerance is critical. It determines the types of stocks or ETFs you should consider investing in and how broadly you should diversify your portfolio.

- **Asset Allocation**: This involves dividing your investment portfolio among different asset categories like stocks, bonds, and other securities. Effective asset allocation is based on the investor's risk tolerance and investment timeline.

- **Diversification**: Diversification is a strategy to reduce risk by spreading investments across various financial instruments, industries, and other categories. It aims to maximize returns by investing in different areas that would each react differently to the same event.

Making Your First Investments

- **Research**: Conduct thorough research or consider consulting with a financial advisor to identify investment opportunities that align with your goals and risk tolerance.

- **Investing vs. Trading**: Decide if you want to be an investor (holding securities for a long term) or a trader (taking advantage of short-term market movements). Your decision will influence your strategy and the types of assets you might purchase.

- **Starting Small**: Consider starting with small amounts and gradually increasing your investment as you gain more confidence and understanding of the market dynamics.

Using Technology and AI Tools

- **Robo-Advisors**: These are automated platforms that use algorithms to manage your investments based on your risk tolerance and goals. They are a good option for beginners due to their low cost and simplicity.

- **Investment Apps**: Many apps today allow beginners to start investing with small amounts of money. They often offer educational resources to help you learn as you go.

- **AI and Machine Learning**: Leverage advanced AI tools for market analysis and investment recommendations. These tools can provide insights derived from massive data sets that are typically not accessible to individual investors.

Monitoring and Adjusting Your Portfolio

- **Regular Reviews**: Regularly review your portfolio to ensure it aligns with your investment goals and risk tolerance. This may involve rebalancing your assets, buying new stocks, or selling underperformers.

- **Stay Informed**: Keep abreast of market trends, economic news, and changes in the financial sector that could impact your investments.

Conclusion

Taking your first steps in the stock market is about laying a solid foundation through education, careful planning, and strategic investment choices. As you become more experienced, you can explore more sophisticated investment strategies and diversify your portfolio further to optimize your returns and minimize risks.

Setting Up Your Investment Account

Getting started with investing requires setting up an investment account through a brokerage. This section will guide you through the process, helping you understand different types of accounts and how to choose the right brokerage.

Choosing a Brokerage

- **Full-Service Brokerages**: These firms offer a wide range of traditional brokerage services including investment advice, financial planning, and portfolio management. They typically charge higher fees but provide personalized service.

- **Discount Brokerages**: Discount brokers provide fewer services but at a lower cost. They are ideal for self-directed investors who prefer to make their own investment decisions.

- **Online Brokerages**: These platforms offer convenient, fast, and often very cost-effective ways to trade stocks. They provide tools for managing your investments digitally, ideal for those comfortable with handling their investment decisions online.

- **Robo-Advisors**: For beginners or those who prefer a hands-off investment strategy, robo-advisors offer automated investment services based on algorithms. They are known for low fees and minimal account balances.

Opening an Investment Account

To open an account, you will typically need to follow these steps:

- **Application**: Fill out an application form, which will include personal identification information, financial history, and investment experience.

- **Verification**: You may need to provide documents to verify your identity, such as a passport, driver's license, or utility bills for proof of address.

- **Funding Your Account**: Once your account is approved, you'll need to fund it. This can be done via bank transfer, check, or even linking your account to other financial institutions.

Understanding Account Types

Investment accounts come in various forms, each suited to different needs and goals:

- **Individual Brokerage Accounts**: Standard accounts for buying and selling securities. Profits are subject to capital gains tax.

- **Joint Accounts**: Operated by two or more individuals, typically used by couples or business partners.

- **Retirement Accounts (IRAs, 401(k)s)**: These offer tax advantages for retirement savings. There are specific rules regarding when you can access these funds without penalties.

- **Education Savings Accounts (ESAs)**: These accounts offer tax-free growth and withdrawals when the funds are used for qualified educational expenses.

- **Custodial Accounts**: Managed by an adult for a minor until they reach adulthood.

Choosing the Right Account

When deciding which type of account to open, consider your financial goals, tax implications, and investment timeline. For instance, if you are saving for retirement, an IRA or a 401(k) might be a better choice due to their tax benefits. For general investing, an individual or joint brokerage account might be suitable.

Tips for Account Setup

- **Understand the Fees**: Be aware of any fees associated with the account, including transaction fees, account management fees, and potential penalties for early withdrawal in the case of retirement accounts.

- **Consider Accessibility**: Choose a brokerage that offers easy access to customer service, robust online tools, and resources that can help you learn and manage your investments effectively.

- **Check for Compatibility**: Ensure that the brokerage's offerings align with your investment strategies, whether you're interested in stocks, ETFs, mutual funds, or other investment vehicles.

How to Buy Your First Stock

Buying your first stock is a significant step in your investment journey. This process can seem complex at first, but by following these steps, you can make your first purchase with confidence.

1. Research and Choose Your Stock

Before making any investment, thorough research is crucial. Consider these factors when choosing a stock:

- **Company Performance**: Look into the company's financial health, profitability, revenue growth, and stability. Financial statements and earnings reports are good starting points.

- **Industry Position**: Evaluate the industry in which the company operates. Is it growing? What are the major challenges and competitors?

- **Market Trends**: Understand broader market trends. How might economic or political factors affect the company?

- **Investment Goals**: Align your stock choice with your investment goals. Are you looking for long-term growth, value investing, or dividend income?

Resources like financial news websites, stock market apps, and investment analysis platforms can provide valuable insights.

2. Set Up a Brokerage Account

If you haven't already set up a brokerage account, you will need to do so (see the previous section, "Setting Up Your Investment Account"). Choose a reputable online broker that aligns with your investment style and needs. Consider factors such as user interface, transaction fees, available resources, and customer support.

3. Fund Your Account

Transfer funds into your brokerage account. Most brokerages offer several funding options, including electronic funds transfers, wire transfers, or checks. Remember, it may take a few days for the funds to be available for trading.

4. Use the Trading Platform

Familiarize yourself with the brokerage's trading platform. Most platforms will allow you to search for stocks by ticker symbol (a unique series of letters assigned to each stock) or by the company name. Spend some time exploring how to place orders, check stock prices, and monitor your portfolio.

5. Place Your Order

Once you've chosen a stock and are ready to buy, you need to place an order. Here are the common types of orders:

- **Market Order**: Buys the stock immediately at the current market price. This is suitable when you want to execute a trade quickly.

- **Limit Order**: Allows you to set a specific price at which you want to buy the stock. The order will only execute if the stock's price reaches or falls below that level. This is useful for buying stocks at a lower price.

- **Stop Order**: Similar to a limit order, but the stock is bought once it reaches a certain price and continues to rise. It's used to limit potential losses or protect gains.

6. Review and Execute

Double-check the details of your order. Make sure you are comfortable with the quantity and price. When ready, execute the trade. Monitor your stock after purchasing to see how it performs relative to your investment expectations and market conditions.

7. Continue Learning

Buying your first stock is just the beginning. Continue educating yourself about the stock market, investment strategies, and portfolio management. Staying informed will help you make smarter investment decisions and adjust your portfolio as needed.

Certainly! Here's a section titled "Essential Tips for New Investors" for Chapter 3 of your book, "No Experience? No Problem! Investing in Stocks with AI Assistance":

Essential Tips for New Investors

Embarking on your investment journey can be exhilarating, but it also comes with its set of challenges. Here are some essential tips to help new investors build a solid foundation for successful investing:

1. Start with a Clear Financial Plan

Before you start investing, it's crucial to have a clear understanding of your financial goals. Are you investing for retirement, to buy a home, or to fund education? Knowing your timeline and objectives will help you determine your investment strategy and risk tolerance.

2. Educate Yourself

Investing without sufficient knowledge can be risky. Take the time to learn the basics of the stock market, different types of investments (stocks, bonds, ETFs), and financial terms. Resources like books, online courses, and financial news websites can be invaluable.

3. Diversify Your Portfolio

Don't put all your eggs in one basket. Diversification helps reduce risk by spreading your investments across various financial instruments, industries, and geographic locations. This strategy can protect your portfolio from volatility and minimize losses during market downturns.

4. Understand Your Risk Tolerance

Risk tolerance is the degree of variability in investment returns that an investor is willing to withstand. Understanding your risk tolerance will guide you in choosing investments that suit your comfort level. Younger investors might take more risks for higher returns, while those closer to retirement may prefer safer, more stable investments.

5. Start Small

It's wise to start with a small amount of money and gradually increase your investment as you gain more confidence and understanding of the market. This approach allows you to learn from your experiences without exposing a significant portion of your capital to risk.

6. Use Technology

Leverage technology to your advantage. Robo-advisors can manage investments based on your risk tolerance and goals at a lower cost than traditional financial advisors. Investment apps and platforms provide tools for tracking and managing your portfolio efficiently.

7. Keep Emotions in Check

Investing can be emotional, particularly when your money is at stake. Avoid making decisions based on short-term market fluctuations. Stay focused on your long-term goals, and don't let fear or greed dictate your actions.

8. Review and Rebalance Regularly

Regularly review your investment portfolio to ensure it still aligns with your goals. Rebalancing by buying or selling assets as needed can help maintain your desired asset allocation and risk level.

9. Plan for Taxes

Understand the tax implications of your investments. Certain accounts like Roth IRAs and 529 plans offer tax advantages that can maximize your returns. Consider consulting with a tax advisor to optimize your investment strategy for tax efficiency.

10. Stay Patient and Committed

Investing is a long-term endeavor. It requires patience and commitment. Markets will fluctuate, but historically, they have trended upward over the long term. Stick with your investment plan, and don't be swayed by short-term uncertainties.

04
INTRODUCTION TO ARTIFICIAL INTELLIGENCE IN INVESTING

As technology advances, artificial intelligence (AI) has become a significant force in many industries, including finance. AI is revolutionizing the way investments are made, offering new opportunities and tools for investors of all levels. This chapter will introduce you to the basics of AI in investing and how it can enhance your investment strategy.

What is Artificial Intelligence?

Artificial Intelligence involves creating computer systems that can perform tasks that typically require human intelligence. These tasks include learning, reasoning, problem-solving, perception, and understanding language. In the context of investing, AI systems are designed to analyze data, recognize patterns, make predictions, and even execute trades at speeds and accuracies that are impossible for humans.

How AI is Used in Investing

1. **Algorithmic Trading**: AI algorithms can execute trades at high speeds based on predefined criteria, such as price movements or trading volume. These algorithms adjust their criteria and

actions based on market conditions without human intervention.

2. **Predictive Analytics**: AI can analyze vast amounts of data to forecast market trends and stock movements. This includes not only structured data, such as market indicators and financial reports but also unstructured data, such as news articles and social media posts.

3. **Portfolio Management**: Robo-advisors use AI to manage and optimize investors' portfolios automatically. They adjust the investments based on the market conditions and the individual's risk preference and financial goals.

4. **Risk Management**: AI tools help identify and assess risk factors by analyzing market data and trends. They provide insights that help investors mitigate potential losses and make more informed decisions.

Benefits of AI in Investing

- **Efficiency**: AI can process information and execute trades much faster than human traders.

- **Accuracy**: By removing emotional bias, AI can make more objective and rational investment decisions.

- **Cost Reduction**: AI systems reduce the need for human labor, which can lower operational costs for investment firms.

- **Accessibility**: AI tools have democratized investing, making advanced trading strategies accessible to individual investors without the need for deep technical knowledge.

Challenges and Considerations

- **Complexity**: AI systems can be complex and difficult to understand, making them less transparent for some investors.

- **Dependence on Data**: AI's effectiveness is heavily dependent on the quality and quantity of data it processes. Poor data can lead to inaccurate predictions and decisions.

- **Regulatory and Ethical Issues**: As AI plays a more significant role in investing, it raises concerns about regulatory compliance, privacy, and the ethical use of AI.

Getting Started with AI in Investing

- **Educate Yourself**: Learn about different AI investing tools and how they work.

- **Start with Robo-Advisors**: Many online platforms offer AI-powered robo-advisors, which can be a good starting point for beginners.

- **Use AI for Analysis**: Use AI tools for data analysis and to gain insights into market conditions, but make final investment decisions based on a comprehensive understanding of the market.

Conclusion

Artificial intelligence is transforming investing by making it more efficient and accessible. While AI can offer significant advantages, it's essential to approach these tools with a clear understanding of both their capabilities and their limitations. As AI technology continues to evolve, staying informed and adaptable will be key to leveraging AI successfully in your investment strategy.

What is Artificial Intelligence?

Artificial Intelligence (AI) refers to the simulation of human intelligence in machines that are programmed to think like humans and mimic their actions. The term may also be applied to any machine that exhibits traits associated with a human mind such as learning and problem-solving. AI is a broad field of study that includes many theories, methods, and technologies, as well as the following major subfields:

Machine Learning

Machine Learning (ML) is a subset of AI that includes algorithms that parse data, learn from that data, and then apply what they have learned to make informed decisions. Essentially, ML systems develop a model based on sample data, known as "training data," in order to make predictions or decisions without being explicitly programmed to perform the task.

Deep Learning

Deep Learning is a type of machine learning that teaches computers to do what comes naturally to humans: learn by example. Deep learning is a key technology behind driverless cars, enabling them to recognize a stop sign, or to distinguish a pedestrian from a lamppost. It is the key technology behind voice control in consumer devices like phones, tablets, TVs, and hands-free speakers.

Natural Language Processing

Natural Language Processing (NLP) involves the ability of computers to understand and process human language. Such capabilities are extremely useful in various applications, such as translating texts from one language to another, responding to voice commands, and summarizing large volumes of text rapidly—even in real-time.

Robotics

Robotics is a field related to AI. Robots are often used to perform tasks that are difficult for humans to perform or perform consistently. They are used in a range of industries including manufacturing, packing and shipping, and servicing orders.

Expert Systems

Expert systems are AI programs that simulate the judgment and behavior of a human or an organization that has expert knowledge and experience in a particular field. These systems are focused on a specific task and use databases of expert knowledge to offer advice or make decisions.

AI Applications in Everyday Life

From smartphone assistants to personalization on streaming services, AI is a part of our daily lives. In the financial sector, AI is used for tasks like quantitative trading, fraud detection, and customer service, and offers substantial improvements in terms of operational efficiency and risk management.

How AI Works

AI systems are powered by algorithms, use databases for knowledge retrieval, and follow patterns in the data to make predictions or suggestions. The performance of these systems improves over time by learning from the outcomes of their actions, in a process known as "training."

How AI is Transforming Investing

Artificial Intelligence (AI) is reshaping the landscape of investing, offering unprecedented capabilities that were once the domain of science fiction. From enhancing decision-making processes to automating complex tasks, AI's impact on investing is profound and multifaceted. Here's how AI is changing the game for investors around the world:

Algorithmic Trading

One of the most significant impacts of AI in investing is in the area of algorithmic trading. AI algorithms can analyze large volumes of data at speeds impossible for humans, executing trades based on complex variables and patterns detected in the market. These algorithms can adapt to new data and alter their trading strategies in real-time, providing a significant edge in terms of speed and efficiency.

Enhanced Market Forecasting

AI excels in identifying patterns from large datasets, including historical price movements, economic reports, and even news events. By using techniques such as machine learning and deep learning, AI models can forecast market trends with greater accuracy than traditional methods. This ability not only helps in predicting stock prices but also in understanding market sentiment and potential future market movements.

Risk Management

AI significantly enhances the ability to analyze and manage risk. By processing and learning from vast amounts of historical data, AI systems can identify potential risk factors that might not be obvious to human analysts. These systems can also simulate different investment scenarios to predict possible outcomes and suggest risk mitigation strategies.

Robo-Advisors

Robo-advisors are AI-driven platforms that provide automated, algorithm-based portfolio management advice without human financial planners. They analyze each investor's financial situation and future goals to offer personalized investment advice. These platforms often come with lower fees than traditional investment advisors, making them accessible to a broader range of investors.

Personalized Investment Solutions

AI enables more personalized investment solutions by analyzing individual investor profiles, including risk tolerance, investment time horizon, and preferences. This allows for more tailored investment strategies that better meet the unique needs of each investor, improving customer satisfaction and investment outcomes.

Operational Efficiency

AI helps financial institutions and investors increase their operational efficiency by automating routine tasks such as data analysis, report generation, and even customer service through chatbots. This automation not only reduces costs but also frees up human resources to focus on more strategic activities.

Legal and Compliance Automation

AI tools can help in monitoring and maintaining compliance with various regulatory requirements. By automatically analyzing communication and transactions, AI can help prevent unethical practices such as insider trading and market manipulation, thus ensuring transparency and fairness in the market.

Challenges and Considerations

While AI brings many benefits, it also presents challenges such as the need for high-quality data, concerns about privacy, and the potential for errors in automated decision-making. Moreover, the increased use of AI in trading can lead to market volatility, as AI-driven trades can amplify market movements.

Benefits of AI for Individual Investors

Artificial Intelligence (AI) is not just a game-changer for institutional investors; it also offers numerous advantages for individual investors. Here are some of the key benefits that AI technologies provide to personal investment strategies:

Improved Decision Making

AI enhances decision-making capabilities by providing deeper and more accurate analyses of data. AI systems can process vast amounts of information—from market data and global economic indicators to social media sentiment—in real-time. This capability allows individual investors to make more informed decisions by having access to insights and analysis that were traditionally available only to professional traders and large financial institutions.

Enhanced Portfolio Management

Robo-advisors, powered by AI, can manage portfolios with a level of sophistication that matches, and sometimes surpasses, human advisors. These systems analyze market conditions, individual investment goals, and risk tolerance to create and manage a diversified portfolio automatically. They can make adjustments in real-time to align with market changes, helping individual investors optimize returns and minimize losses.

Access to Sophisticated Investment Strategies

AI democratizes access to complex investment strategies that were once the preserve of hedge funds and elite investors. Techniques such as algorithmic trading and machine learning models for predictive analytics are now available through platforms that cater to individual investors, allowing them to employ strategies that can dynamically adapt to changing market conditions.

Cost Efficiency

AI-driven investment tools often come with lower fees compared to traditional investment management services. By automating various functions, such as transaction execution and portfolio rebalancing, AI reduces the need for human labor, which in turn lowers the cost for investors. This cost efficiency makes investing more accessible to a broader audience and allows individual investors to keep a larger portion of their returns.

Risk Reduction

One of the standout advantages of AI in investing is its ability to identify and assess risk more accurately. AI systems use historical data and pattern recognition to forecast potential downturns and suggest preventative measures. For individual investors, this means better protection against volatility and market downturns, which can help preserve capital in uncertain times.

Real-Time Monitoring and Alerts

AI systems can monitor portfolios and market movements around the clock, providing real-time alerts to investors about critical changes or opportunities. This level of monitoring ensures that individual investors can react quickly to market developments, a capability especially valuable in today's fast-paced financial markets.

Personalized Financial Planning

AI can tailor financial advice and investment strategies to the specific needs and goals of individual investors. By analyzing personal financial data and life goals, AI-driven platforms can offer customized advice that aligns with long-term financial planning, including retirement planning, savings goals, and investment preferences.

Continuous Learning and Adaptation

AI systems are designed to learn from data continuously, which means they can improve their predictions and strategies over time. For individual investors, this results in progressively smarter advice and more refined investment strategies that adapt as market conditions change and as personal financial situations evolve.

05
AI TOOLS AND PLATFORMS FOR INVESTORS

As artificial intelligence (AI) continues to evolve, a wide range of AI-driven tools and platforms have emerged, transforming how individual investors manage their portfolios, make trades, and analyze markets. This chapter explores various AI tools and platforms that can help investors harness the power of AI to enhance their investment strategies.

Robo-Advisors

Robo-advisors are perhaps the most widely recognized AI tools in the investment world. These platforms use algorithms to automatically manage and optimize an investor's portfolio based on their risk tolerance and investment goals. Some popular robo-advisors include:

- **Betterment**: Known for its goal-based investment strategies and tax-loss harvesting capabilities.
- **Wealthfront**: Offers a wide range of investment accounts and features like direct indexing.
- **Ellevest**: Tailored specifically towards women, focusing on unique salary curves and lifespan considerations.

Algorithmic Trading Platforms

Algorithmic trading platforms use AI to execute trades at high speeds and volumes based on predefined criteria. These platforms are particularly useful for day traders and those who engage in high-frequency trading. Examples include:

- **QuantConnect**: Provides a platform for designing and testing algorithmic trading strategies in equities, forex, and cryptocurrencies.//
- **MetaTrader 4/5**: Popular for forex and CFD trading, these platforms allow users to implement custom trading robots (Expert Advisors) to automate trading.

Predictive Analytics Tools

These tools use machine learning models to predict market trends and stock movements. They analyze historical data and market indicators to forecast future performance, helping investors make more informed decisions. Some tools in this category include:

- **Yewno|Edge**: Offers insights by transforming vast amounts of data into actionable knowledge, including forecasts and trends.
- **TipRanks**: Aggregates data from analysts, hedge funds, and thousands of news sources to provide investor sentiment and price forecasts.

Portfolio Management Software

AI-driven portfolio management software helps investors track and manage their assets efficiently, providing insights into asset allocation, portfolio balancing, and potential investment opportunities. Notable examples include:

- **Personal Capital**: Combines automated investing with access to financial advisors.
- **SigFig**: Manages portfolios by using algorithms to analyze and adjust the investments automatically.

Sentiment Analysis Tools

These platforms analyze sentiments in news articles, social media, and financial blogs to gauge market sentiment towards certain stocks or the market in general. This can be particularly useful for understanding the potential impact of public sentiment on market movements. Examples include:

- **Accern**: Uses AI to monitor news and social media in real-time to detect early stories relevant to investors.
- **StockPulse**: Specializes in emotion data analysis for finance, providing insights into investor sentiment.

AI Chatbots for Personal Finance

AI chatbots can assist with basic investment queries and customer service tasks, offering a conversational interface that can guide new investors through the complexities of finance. Examples include:

- **Charles Schwab's Schwab Assistant**: Allows users to inquire about stock prices, trade equities, and access accounts through voice commands.
- **Plum**: An AI assistant that helps save money and invest it automatically into portfolios.

Conclusion

AI tools and platforms offer a range of functionalities that can significantly enhance an investor's ability to manage their finances and investments effectively. Whether it's through making more informed decisions, automating portfolio management, or analyzing vast amounts of market data, AI is a powerful ally in the quest to maximize investment returns. As these technologies continue to develop, they will provide even deeper insights and more refined tools for personal investment management.

Overview of Popular AI Investment Tools

AI investment tools are transforming the landscape of investing by automating complex processes and offering insights derived from large datasets. Here are some widely used AI tools that cater to various aspects of investing:

Robo-Advisors

Betterment
One of the pioneers in robo-advising, Betterment uses advanced algorithms to manage portfolios, optimize asset allocation, and perform tax-loss harvesting, all based on the user's risk tolerance and goals.

Wealthfront
Wealthfront provides a comprehensive automated investing service that includes stock level tax-loss harvesting, financial planning, and portfolio rebalancing. It uses sophisticated algorithms to tailor advice and management based on personal financial situations.

Algorithmic Trading Software

QuantConnect
An open-source, cloud-based algorithmic trading platform that allows users to design, backtest, and execute trading strategies across multiple asset classes including equities, options, futures, and cryptocurrencies.

MetaTrader 5
A popular platform for forex and CFD trading, MetaTrader 5 allows users to run and test automated trading strategies using its proprietary scripting language, MQL5. It supports both backtesting and real-time trading.

Predictive Analytics and Market Forecasting Tools

TipRanks
This tool aggregates financial data and analyst predictions to provide retail investors with a clearer view of the expected performance of stocks and the reliability of financial experts who provide those predictions.

TradingView
TradingView combines social networking with stock trading and investing. It includes tools for chart analysis, which is enriched with AI-driven insights to predict market movements and trends.

Sentiment Analysis Tools

Accern
Accern accelerates AI workflows for financial services with a no-code development platform. It analyzes news articles and social media to monitor sentiment and recognize patterns that could impact markets and specific stocks.

StockGeist.ai
This platform monitors public sentiment in real-time from news sources and social media to gauge public mood about specific stocks. It provides a dashboard that visualizes sentiment analysis to aid in decision-making.

Portfolio Management

Personal Capital

Personal Capital combines automated investing with personal financial advice. Its technology provides users with a detailed view of their investments and an analysis of how to optimize their financial strategy.

SigFig

SigFig specializes in portfolio tracking and management. It uses algorithms to analyze and optimize users' existing portfolios and suggest improvements based on efficiency and fee reduction.

Comprehensive Investment Platforms

Interactive Brokers

Known for its robust trading technology, Interactive Brokers incorporates AI in many of its tools to provide investors with advanced trading capabilities, risk management, and research tools.

Schwab Intelligent Portfolios

Offered by Charles Schwab, these are automated investment portfolios that adjust according to the markets and the investor's goals, using algorithms to rebalance assets as needed.

How to Use Robo-Advisors

Robo-advisors are automated online platforms that provide financial planning services with minimal human intervention. They utilize sophisticated algorithms to manage and optimize clients' portfolios based on their financial goals and risk tolerance. Here's a guide on how to use robo-advisors effectively:

Step 1: Select a Robo-Advisor

When choosing a robo-advisor, consider factors such as investment strategies, fees, minimum investment requirements, and the types of accounts offered (e.g., taxable, IRA, etc.). Popular robo-advisors include Betterment, Wealthfront, and Schwab Intelligent Portfolios. Research and compare different services to find the one that best fits your needs.

Step 2: Set Up Your Account

Setting up an account typically involves filling out an online application on the robo-advisor's website. You'll be asked to provide personal information and complete a questionnaire about your investment goals, financial situation, and risk tolerance. This information helps the robo-advisor understand your objectives and design a suitable investment strategy.

Step 3: Fund Your Account

Once your account is set up, you will need to fund it. Most robo-advisors support funding through bank transfers. Some might also allow funding via check or rollover from another retirement account. Check the specific funding options available with your chosen robo-advisor.

Step 4: Understand Your Investment Plan

After your account is funded, the robo-advisor will propose an investment plan based on your profile. This plan usually includes a suggested asset allocation and selection of investment vehicles, such as ETFs. Review this plan to ensure it aligns with your expectations and adjust the risk level if necessary.

Step 5: Portfolio Management

The robo-advisor will automatically manage your portfolio. This includes rebalancing the assets to maintain the target allocation, reinvesting dividends, and potentially harvesting tax losses to optimize your tax situation. You can monitor your portfolio through the platform's dashboard, which provides insights into your investments and performance metrics.

Step 6: Adjustments and Updates

Life changes, and so may your financial goals or risk tolerance. It's important to update your information in the robo-advisor platform if your financial situation or goals change. The robo-advisor will adjust your portfolio accordingly to stay aligned with your new objectives.

Step 7: Review Performance

Regularly review the performance of your investments with the robo-advisor to ensure they are on track to meet your financial goals. Most platforms provide detailed reports and analytics to help you understand your portfolio's performance against market benchmarks.

Benefits of Using Robo-Advisors

- **Cost-Effective**: Robo-advisors typically charge lower fees than traditional financial advisors.

- **Efficient**: Automated management means your portfolio is continually monitored and adjusted without needing your direct intervention.

- **Accessible**: Easy to use and accessible from anywhere with an internet connection, making investing straightforward for beginners.

Considerations

- **Limited Personalization**: While robo-advisors handle standard investment scenarios well, they may not fully account for more complex financial situations or preferences.

- **Dependency on Technology**: As with any automated system, there's a dependency on the underlying technology, which may have limitations or vulnerabilities.

AI-Powered Stock Analysis and Prediction Tools

Artificial Intelligence (AI) has revolutionized stock analysis and prediction by enabling faster, more accurate assessments of market data and trends. These tools use sophisticated algorithms and machine learning techniques to predict stock price movements, analyze market conditions, and provide actionable insights. Here's an overview of how AI-powered stock analysis and prediction tools work and their benefits for investors.

Types of AI-Powered Tools

1. **Machine Learning Models**: These tools use historical data to train models that can predict future stock prices or market trends. They adjust their predictions based on new data, improving their accuracy over time.

2. **Natural Language Processing (NLP)**: NLP tools analyze textual data from news articles, financial reports, and social media to gauge market sentiment. They can identify positive or negative sentiments that may affect stock prices.

3. **Neural Networks**: Particularly deep learning models, these are used for more complex predictions such as identifying patterns

in stock price movements that are not immediately obvious to human analysts.

Popular AI-Powered Stock Analysis Tools

- **Trade Ideas**: This tool uses AI to scan the stock market in real-time and identify high-probability trading opportunities. It offers automated trading alongside personalized trading insights.

- **Sentieo**: Combines traditional financial data with alternative data sources like social media sentiment to provide comprehensive stock analysis. Sentieo employs NLP to sift through enormous volumes of data to detect market-moving trends.

- **TrendSpider**: This technical analysis software uses AI to help traders build smarter trading plans. It automates the analysis of technical indicators and candlestick patterns.

How to Use AI-Powered Tools for Stock Prediction

1. **Data Input**: Provide the tool with access to relevant data sources. This could include historical stock prices, financial statements, market data, and news feeds.

2. **Analysis and Model Building**: The AI tool analyzes the data to identify patterns or trends. Many platforms allow users to customize the parameters of the prediction models according to their trading strategies.

3. **Receive Predictions and Insights**: The tool offers predictions about future stock behavior or market trends. Some tools also provide confidence scores indicating how reliable a particular prediction might be.

4. **Incorporate into Trading Strategy**: Use these insights as part of your broader trading strategy. AI-generated predictions should be one of several tools used in decision-making, combined with fundamental analysis and personal insight.

Benefits of Using AI in Stock Analysis

- **Speed and Efficiency**: AI can analyze vast amounts of data much faster than human analysts, providing timely insights that are critical in fast-moving markets.

- **Accuracy**: By learning from vast historical data sets, AI models can make highly accurate predictions that might elude even experienced traders.

- **Objective Analysis**: AI tools are not influenced by human emotions, which can lead to biased decisions. Their objective analysis helps maintain a consistent approach to trading.

Challenges

- **Dependency on Data Quality**: The accuracy of AI predictions heavily depends on the quality and comprehensiveness of the input data.

- **Overreliance**: There's a risk of over-relying on AI tools. Successful investing requires a balanced approach that includes qualitative analysis and human judgment.

- **Complexity**: Some AI tools can be complex to set up and require a steep learning curve to understand and use effectively.

06
MAKING SMART INVESTMENT CHOICES WITH AI

As artificial intelligence (AI) technologies become increasingly sophisticated, they offer individual investors powerful tools for making smarter investment choices. This chapter explores how AI can be integrated into your investment strategy to enhance decision-making, improve returns, and manage risks more effectively.

Understanding AI-Enabled Investment Strategies

AI-driven investment strategies utilize algorithms to analyze market data, predict trends, and make investment decisions. These strategies can range from simple automated advisory services to complex trading algorithms used in high-frequency trading. The key to leveraging AI in investing is understanding how these technologies work and how they can be applied to meet your investment goals.

Integrating AI into Your Investment Process

1. **Goal Setting**: Start by clearly defining your investment goals and risk tolerance. AI tools can then help tailor your investment strategy to align with these goals, optimizing your asset allocation and portfolio diversification.

2. **Data Analysis**: AI excels in analyzing vast amounts of data quickly and accurately. Use AI tools to gather and process data

from various sources, including market trends, economic indicators, and corporate financial statements, to inform your investment decisions.

3. **Predictive Analytics**: Employ AI-driven predictive analytics to forecast market movements and identify potential investment opportunities. These tools use historical data and machine learning techniques to predict future price movements of stocks, bonds, and other securities.

4. **Risk Assessment and Management**: AI can help identify and assess potential risks, providing insights into factors that could impact your investments. Use AI to simulate different market scenarios and their potential impact on your portfolio, allowing you to make informed decisions on risk management.

5. **Portfolio Optimization**: AI algorithms can continuously monitor and adjust your portfolio to ensure it remains aligned with your investment strategy. This includes automatic rebalancing, identifying underperforming assets, and suggesting changes to maximize returns and minimize risks.

AI Tools for Making Smart Investment Choices

- **Robo-Advisors**: Platforms like Betterment and Wealthfront analyze your financial situation and automatically manage your investments, providing a hands-off approach to portfolio management.

- **AI Trading Bots**: Tools like Algoriz allow investors to write trading algorithms without coding, using natural language processing to execute trades based on specified criteria.

- **Sentiment Analysis Tools**: Platforms like StockPulse and Accern analyze social media and news to gauge market sentiment, helping investors understand public perception of potential investments.

Best Practices for Using AI in Investing

- **Stay Informed**: Keep up-to-date with the latest developments in AI technology and investment strategies. Understanding the tools you're using is crucial for leveraging them effectively.

- **Maintain Oversight**: While AI can automate many aspects of the investment process, maintain oversight and periodically review the decisions made by AI systems to ensure they align with your overall investment strategy.

- **Balance AI with Human Judgment**: AI should complement, not replace, human judgment. Use AI as a tool to aid decision-making but rely on your judgment and consultation with financial advisors to make final investment decisions.

Conclusion

AI offers a range of tools and technologies that can significantly enhance investment strategies. By understanding and integrating AI into your investment process, you can make smarter, more informed investment choices that align with your financial goals and risk tolerance. As AI continues to evolve, staying adaptive and informed will be key to leveraging these technologies effectively in the ever-changing investment landscape.

How AI Can Help You Choose Stocks

Artificial Intelligence (AI) has dramatically changed the landscape for individual investors by providing powerful tools to analyze and select stocks. AI enhances traditional stock picking techniques with speed, efficiency, and an unprecedented depth of analysis. Here's how AI can be an invaluable tool in helping you choose the right stocks:

Automated Analysis of Financial Data

AI algorithms excel at processing vast amounts of financial data rapidly. This includes quarterly earnings reports, balance sheets, cash flow statements, and more. AI can analyze this data to provide insights about a company's financial health, growth trajectory, and potential risks much faster than a human analyst could.

Predictive Analytics

AI leverages machine learning models to predict future stock performance based on historical data. These models consider various factors such as past price movements, trading volumes, industry performance, and economic indicators. By identifying patterns and trends that may not be apparent to the human eye, AI provides forecasts and predictive insights, helping investors make informed decisions about which stocks to consider.

Sentiment Analysis

Sentiment analysis uses natural language processing (NLP) to interpret and quantify the emotional tone behind qualitative information. This includes news articles, social media posts, analyst reports, and other public communications about a company or the market. AI tools assess this sentiment to gauge public perception and potential market reactions, which can influence stock prices.

Enhanced Risk Assessment

AI can identify risk factors more efficiently by analyzing market conditions and external factors that might affect stock prices. This includes geopolitical events, changes in regulatory landscapes, and shifts in consumer behavior. By understanding these risks, investors can make more informed decisions about which stocks to buy or avoid.

Portfolio Diversification

AI also assists in creating a diversified investment portfolio. It can analyze the correlation between different stocks and sectors, recommending a mix that minimizes risk while aiming to maximize returns. This helps investors spread out potential risks and take advantage of different market conditions.

Real-Time Market Monitoring

AI tools continuously monitor market conditions and update their analyses in real time. This enables them to provide timely recommendations that reflect the latest market trends and data. For investors, this means having up-to-date information that can influence buying or selling decisions to optimize investment outcomes.

Algorithmic Trading Strategies

For more advanced users, AI can power algorithmic trading strategies that automate the buying and selling of stocks based on predefined criteria. These systems can execute trades at optimal times based on market conditions, helping to capitalize on short-term price fluctuations and market inefficiencies.

How to Leverage AI for Stock Selection

1. **Choose the Right Tools**: Research and select AI tools that best meet your investment style and needs.
2. **Combine with Fundamental Analysis**: While AI provides powerful insights, combining these with traditional

fundamental analysis ensures a well-rounded approach to stock selection.

3. **Set Clear Objectives**: Define clear investment objectives and risk tolerance to guide the AI in selecting stocks that fit your portfolio.

4. **Monitor and Adjust**: Regularly review the AI's performance and the resulting stock picks. Be prepared to adjust your strategies as market conditions change.

Integrating AI into Your Investment Strategy

Artificial Intelligence (AI) is not just a tool for automating tasks but a transformative technology that can significantly enhance your investment strategy. Integrating AI into your investing processes involves understanding how it can augment decision-making, improve efficiency, and provide a competitive edge. Here's how you can seamlessly incorporate AI technologies into your investment activities:

Understand AI Capabilities and Limitations

Before integrating AI into your strategy, it's important to understand what AI can and cannot do. AI excels at processing large volumes of data, identifying patterns, and making predictions based on historical information. However, AI is only as good as the data it receives and may not fully grasp nuances that a human investor might consider, such as unexpected market or political events. Understanding these capabilities and limitations will help you leverage AI effectively without over-relying on it.

Start with a Clear Investment Framework

Define your investment goals, risk tolerance, and time horizon. These parameters will guide how you implement AI tools. For instance, if your focus is long-term growth, you might use AI for portfolio management and asset allocation. If you're a day trader, on the other hand, algorithmic trading tools might be more appropriate.

Choose the Right AI Tools

There are various AI tools available, each suited to different aspects of investing:

- **Robo-advisors** for automated portfolio management and rebalancing.

- **Algorithmic trading platforms** for executing high-speed trades based on technical indicators.

- **Predictive analytics tools** for forecasting market trends and stock performance.

- **Sentiment analysis software** for gauging market sentiment from social media and news.

Select tools that align with your investment strategy and can integrate seamlessly into your existing processes.

Data-Driven Decision Making

Incorporate AI tools that enhance your ability to make data-driven decisions. This could mean using AI to analyze financial statements, market data, and economic reports more efficiently. AI can also help identify investment opportunities by detecting subtle patterns or changes in market conditions that might not be visible to the naked eye.

Continuously Monitor and Adjust

AI is continually evolving, and so should your investment strategy. Regularly review and adjust your AI tools and strategies based on performance outcomes and changing market conditions. This includes tweaking algorithms, introducing new data sets, or even pausing certain AI functionalities during volatile market periods.

Combine AI Insights with Human Judgment

While AI can process information and provide recommendations, human judgment is invaluable, especially in understanding context and ethical considerations. Use AI as a tool to aid your decision-making process, but always review AI-generated advice through the lens of your own investment knowledge and intuition.

Educate Yourself Continuously

AI and machine learning are rapidly advancing fields. Staying educated on the latest developments and understanding how new technologies can impact investment is crucial. Consider attending seminars, subscribing to relevant publications, and participating in online forums dedicated to AI investing.

Legal and Ethical Considerations

Ensure that your use of AI adheres to all relevant laws and ethical guidelines. This includes respecting data privacy, avoiding biased data sets, and ensuring that your investment decisions are transparent and accountable.

Case Studies: AI Success Stories

Artificial Intelligence (AI) has revolutionized various aspects of investing, providing significant advantages to those who have embraced its capabilities. The following case studies highlight how AI has successfully been integrated into investment strategies, yielding impressive results.

Case Study 1: Enhancing Portfolio Management with Robo-Advisors

Background: Betterment, one of the leading robo-advisors, utilizes AI to manage portfolios for thousands of clients, optimizing for tax efficiency and tailored risk tolerance.

Strategy: Betterment uses AI algorithms to automatically balance and rebalance clients' portfolios based on real-time market data and individual investor profiles. This includes strategic tax-loss harvesting and adjusting the asset mix as per changing market conditions and client goals.

Outcome: The AI-driven approach has allowed Betterment to significantly outperform traditional investment strategies, especially in volatile markets, by minimizing tax liabilities and ensuring optimal asset allocation.

Case Study 2: Algorithmic Trading in Action

Background: Quantitative trading firm Renaissance Technologies, known for its secrecy and technical prowess, employs complex mathematical models and machine learning to predict market changes more accurately than traditional investment strategies.

Strategy: The firm's Medallion Fund uses proprietary trading algorithms that process massive amounts of data to identify profitable trading opportunities across multiple markets and instruments, executing trades at high speeds.

Outcome: The Medallion Fund is famously successful, often achieving annual returns exceeding 30%, significantly outperforming the market and demonstrating the power of AI in high-frequency trading.

Case Study 3: AI-Powered Sentiment Analysis for Market Prediction

Background: A technology startup developed an AI tool capable of performing sentiment analysis by scanning thousands of news articles, tweets, and financial reports within minutes.

Strategy: The AI tool analyzes the sentiment expressed in the media about specific stocks and the stock market overall, providing investors with insights into public perception and potential market movements before they become apparent through traditional analysis.

Outcome: Investors using this tool were able to anticipate and react to a major market move based on a negative sentiment trend identified by AI before it was reflected in stock prices, securing profits and avoiding losses.

Case Study 4: Deep Learning for Long-Term Investment

Background: An investment firm incorporated deep learning models to analyze historical data from the past 50 years to identify long-term investment opportunities and risks.

Strategy: The firm's deep learning model analyzed patterns in global economic indicators, corporate performance metrics, and historical market data to predict future trends and asset performance.

Outcome: This predictive capability allowed the firm to make strategic long-term investments that yielded high returns over time, significantly outperforming benchmarks.

Lessons Learned

These case studies illustrate several key points about the use of AI in investing:

- **Diverse Applications**: AI can be effectively applied across different areas of investing, from portfolio management to algorithmic trading and market sentiment analysis.

- **Continuous Improvement**: AI systems improve over time as they process more data, making them increasingly valuable as predictive tools.

- **Human Oversight**: While AI provides powerful tools for analysis and execution, human oversight remains crucial, particularly in strategy formulation and risk management.

07
MANAGING YOUR INVESTMENT PORTFOLIO

Effective portfolio management is critical to achieving long-term financial goals while minimizing risk. This chapter explores how investors can actively manage their investment portfolios, with a focus on utilizing AI technologies to enhance these processes.

Portfolio Management Basics

Portfolio management involves constructing and maintaining an investment portfolio aligned with an investor's financial goals, risk tolerance, and investment horizon. It includes:

- **Asset Allocation**: Distributing investments across various asset classes (e.g., stocks, bonds, real estate) to achieve a balance between risk and return.

- **Diversification**: Spreading investments within each asset class to reduce risk.

- **Rebalancing**: Adjusting the portfolio periodically to maintain the original asset allocation, which can drift due to differing returns from various assets.

Integrating AI in Portfolio Management

AI can transform traditional portfolio management through automation and sophisticated analysis, providing the following benefits:

1. **Automated Rebalancing**: AI-driven tools like robo-advisors automatically rebalance portfolios to keep them aligned with investors' target asset allocations, responding dynamically to market shifts.

2. **Optimized Asset Allocation**: Using predictive analytics and machine learning, AI can suggest optimal asset allocation based on projected market conditions and individual investor profiles.

3. **Risk Assessment**: AI models can analyze vast amounts of data to identify potential risks and suggest mitigation strategies, tailoring these insights to the specifics of an investor's portfolio.

4. **Performance Analysis**: AI tools provide detailed analytics on portfolio performance, including comparisons to benchmarks, historical performance simulation, and advanced metrics like Sharpe ratio or alpha generation.

Steps for AI-Enhanced Portfolio Management

1. **Define Objectives and Constraints**: Clearly outline your financial goals, risk tolerance, investment horizon, and any specific preferences or constraints.

2. **Select AI Tools**: Choose AI tools that align with your investment strategy. Consider tools that offer comprehensive features including automated rebalancing, tax optimization, and detailed performance reports.

3. **Input Accurate Data**: Ensure that all relevant financial data is accurately inputted into the AI system. This includes current holdings, transaction history, tax information, and any other relevant financial data.

4. **Monitor AI Recommendations**: Regularly review the recommendations and adjustments suggested by AI tools. While AI can provide powerful insights, it's important to remain engaged and ensure these recommendations align with your overall investment strategy.

5. **Stay Informed on AI Developments**: Keep up-to-date with advancements in AI technology that could impact investment strategies. This includes new tools, enhanced algorithms, or changes in regulatory frameworks affecting AI usage in investing.

6. **Continuously Adjust**: As your financial situation or market conditions change, adjust your inputs and settings in your AI tools to reflect these changes. Regularly revisiting your strategy will help ensure it remains effective and aligned with your goals.

Ethical and Practical Considerations

While integrating AI into portfolio management offers numerous advantages, it's crucial to consider ethical implications such as data privacy, potential biases in AI algorithms, and the transparency of AI decision-making processes. Additionally, investors should be aware of over-reliance on AI tools and ensure that human oversight remains a central component of the investment process.

Portfolio Management Basics

Effective portfolio management is essential for meeting your financial goals and managing investment risks. Whether you're saving for retirement, building wealth, or generating income, understanding the fundamentals of portfolio management can help you make informed investment decisions. This section covers the key concepts and strategies involved in managing an investment portfolio.

Understanding Asset Allocation

Asset allocation involves dividing an investment portfolio among different asset categories, such as stocks, bonds, real estate, and cash. The process is crucial because it has a major impact on your portfolio's risk and return profile. The allocation should reflect your risk tolerance, investment horizon, and financial goals.

- **Stocks** offer potential for high returns but come with higher volatility.
- **Bonds** provide regular income and are generally less volatile than stocks.
- **Real Estate** can offer both income through rent and potential appreciation in value.
- **Cash and equivalents** offer low returns but high liquidity and safety.

The right asset mix balances the potential for higher returns against the risk of losses, aiming to achieve your financial objectives within your comfort level for risk.

The Importance of Diversification

Diversification is a strategy to reduce risk by spreading investments across various financial instruments, industries, and other categories. By diversifying, you can reduce the impact of poor performance in any single investment on the overall portfolio. For example, stock market volatility might affect stocks, but not bonds or real estate, and vice versa. Diversification is often summed up as, "Don't put all your eggs in one basket."

Regular Rebalancing

Rebalancing is the process of realigning the weightings of a portfolio's assets. Rebalancing ensures that the portfolio remains aligned with the investor's intended asset allocation, reducing risk and maintaining the portfolio's original risk-return profile over time. This might involve:

- Buying more of assets that have decreased in relative value.
- Selling off assets that have increased in relative value.

For instance, if your target allocation was 60% stocks and 40% bonds, and due to market movements, your stocks now represent 70% of your portfolio, you would sell some stocks and buy more bonds to get back to your target allocation.

Using Benchmarks

Benchmarks are standard indices used to measure the performance of an investment portfolio. For example, a portfolio of U.S. stocks might be compared to the S&P 500 index. Benchmarks help investors gauge the performance of their investments relative to the broader market or similar assets. This assessment can inform decisions about whether to adjust the strategy or continue on the same path.

Implementing Portfolio Management

To implement these basics into managing your portfolio:

1. **Assess Your Financial Situation**: Understand your current financial situation, risk tolerance, and investment objectives.

2. **Choose the Right Asset Allocation**: Based on your assessment, allocate your investments across different asset categories.

3. **Diversify Your Investments**: Within each asset category, diversify your holdings to spread risk.

4. **Monitor and Rebalance**: Regularly review your portfolio's performance against your goals and rebalance as needed.

5. **Use Benchmarks**: Compare your portfolio's performance with relevant benchmarks to evaluate its effectiveness.

How AI Can Optimize Your Portfolio

Artificial Intelligence (AI) is becoming an integral tool in modern portfolio management, providing innovative solutions for optimizing asset allocation, managing risks, and enhancing overall investment performance. Here's how AI technologies can help you refine and optimize your investment portfolio:

Enhanced Asset Allocation

AI can analyze vast amounts of data quickly and predict future market trends with high accuracy, allowing for more dynamic and responsive asset allocation. By incorporating machine learning algorithms, AI can:

- **Identify Patterns**: Uncover subtle patterns and correlations in the market data that might be missed by traditional analysis.

- **Adapt to Market Changes**: Continuously learn from new data, enabling real-time adjustments to the portfolio to better align with market conditions.
- **Personalize Portfolios**: Tailor asset allocations based on individual risk profiles and investment goals, adapting to changes in an investor's life circumstances or financial objectives.

Automated Rebalancing

Rebalancing a portfolio can be tedious and time-consuming, especially for individual investors managing their own investments. AI automates this process by:

- **Monitoring Asset Weights**: Keeping track of the actual asset allocation and comparing it with the target allocation.
- **Triggering Trades**: Automatically executing trades to realign the portfolio with the desired asset allocation, ensuring that the portfolio remains balanced and diversified.
- **Minimizing Costs**: Executing rebalancing at optimal times to reduce transaction costs and tax implications.

Risk Management

Effective risk management is crucial for long-term investment success. AI enhances risk assessment and management by:

- **Predicting Volatility**: Using historical and real-time data to forecast market volatility, allowing investors to adjust their portfolios in anticipation of market downturns.
- **Stress Testing**: Simulating various economic scenarios to see how the portfolio would perform under different conditions, helping to identify potential vulnerabilities.

- **Risk Factor Analysis**: Analyzing a multitude of risk factors simultaneously, including credit risk, market risk, and liquidity risk, and suggesting mitigation strategies.

Predictive Analytics

AI's predictive capabilities are perhaps its most significant benefit for portfolio optimization. By forecasting future movements and trends in the market, AI can:

- **Optimize Returns**: Identify potentially high-performing investments before they become apparent to the market.
- **Reduce Downtime**: Predict downtrends or losses, allowing for proactive adjustments to minimize losses.
- **Enhance Timing**: Improve the timing of buying and selling decisions to maximize investment gains.

Continuous Learning and Improvement

AI systems are designed to improve over time through continuous learning processes, which means they can adapt and evolve with the financial markets. This adaptability leads to:

- **Refined Strategies**: As AI systems learn from past successes and failures, they refine their algorithms to make better predictions and investment decisions.
- **Customized Advice**: AI can adjust its recommendations based on an investor's feedback and changing market conditions, providing highly personalized investment advice.

Implementation Considerations

To effectively integrate AI into your portfolio management strategy, consider the following:

- **Choose Reliable AI Tools**: Opt for AI platforms with proven track records and robust security measures.

- **Understand the Underlying Models**: Have a basic understanding of how the AI makes its decisions and the data it uses.

- **Balance AI and Human Oversight**: Use AI as a tool to aid decision-making, not replace it. Combine AI insights with personal judgment and external advice from financial experts.

When to Buy and Sell: AI Insights

Determining the optimal times to buy and sell securities is crucial for successful investing. Artificial Intelligence (AI) can significantly enhance this decision-making process by providing insights based on data analysis, trend prediction, and market timing strategies. Here's how AI can help you decide when to buy and sell investments:

AI-Driven Market Analysis

AI technologies utilize advanced algorithms to analyze market data and identify trends that are not immediately obvious. This analysis includes:

- **Historical Data Review**: AI systems analyze years of market data to identify long-term trends and patterns.

- **Real-Time Market Sentiment**: AI tools equipped with natural language processing can analyze news articles, social media feeds, and financial reports to gauge market sentiment.

- **Predictive Analytics**: Using machine learning, AI predicts future price movements based on historical and current data trends.

AI Recommendations for Buying

AI can suggest the best times to buy stocks or other assets by identifying:

- **Underpriced Assets**: AI analyzes financial metrics and market conditions to find assets that are undervalued compared to their intrinsic value.

- **Market Entry Points**: Based on volatility and market cycle analysis, AI can suggest optimal entry points for long-term investment success.

- **Sector Opportunities**: AI can identify sectors or industries showing signs of growth before they become mainstream knowledge.

AI Insights on Selling

Conversely, AI also provides valuable insights on when it might be wise to sell an asset:

- **Risk of Decline**: If an asset is predicted to decrease in value based on market trends or deteriorating company fundamentals, AI can recommend selling before the decline.

- **Profit Maximization**: AI can suggest selling points based on profit-taking levels pre-determined by the investor's risk tolerance and investment goals.

- **Portfolio Rebalancing**: AI systems monitor portfolio diversification and can recommend selling certain assets to maintain balance according to the investor's strategy.

Automated Trading

Some AI tools can automate the buying and selling process:

- **Algorithmic Trading**: These systems execute trades at optimal times based on user-defined criteria, reducing the emotion and hesitation often associated with manual trading.

- **Stop-Loss and Take-Profit Orders**: AI can manage these orders to automatically close positions at predefined prices, helping to lock in profits and limit losses.

Integrating AI Insights with Human Judgment

While AI provides powerful tools for analyzing data and predicting market trends, successful investing also requires human judgment. Consider these practices:

- **Review AI Recommendations**: Always review AI suggestions and analyze the reasoning behind them before executing any trades.

- **Stay Informed**: Keep abreast of global economic news and sector-specific developments that might affect your investments. AI may not fully account for sudden economic changes or geopolitical events.

- **Monitor AI Performance**: Regularly assess the performance of your AI tools to ensure they are achieving your investment objectives. Adjust parameters as needed to align with your strategy.

Conclusion

AI offers profound insights into the optimal times to buy and sell securities, enhancing investors' abilities to make informed decisions. By leveraging AI-driven analytics and combining them with personal investment knowledge and real-world awareness, investors can optimize their trading strategies for better outcomes.

08
ADVANCED AI INVESTING TECHNIQUES

As AI technology evolves, it brings sophisticated tools that can significantly enhance investment strategies. This chapter delves into advanced AI investing techniques that leverage complex algorithms and machine learning to uncover deeper insights, optimize investment strategies, and increase potential returns.

Algorithmic Trading

Algorithmic Trading involves using computer programs to make high-speed trading decisions to capitalize on market efficiencies and arbitrage opportunities. Here's how AI powers this advanced technique:

- **High-Frequency Trading (HFT)**: AI-driven HFT strategies can execute thousands of orders at lightning speeds, taking advantage of very small price gaps and trading volume data.
- **Statistical Arbitrage**: AI algorithms analyze historical price relationships between stocks to identify and exploit pricing inefficiencies.
- **Market Making**: AI systems can act as market makers, using algorithms to provide liquidity in the markets, earning profits on the bid-ask spread.

Predictive Analytics

Predictive Analytics uses AI to forecast future market behaviors based on historical data. This technique involves:

- **Time Series Analysis**: AI models analyze time-series data to predict future stock price movements based on patterns observed in the past.

- **Sentiment Analysis**: Utilizing NLP, AI assesses the mood and opinions expressed in news articles, blogs, and social media to predict their impact on market movements.

- **Event-Driven Trading**: AI systems can be trained to react to specific market-moving events, such as economic announcements or earnings reports, and make calculated trading decisions based on predicted outcomes.

Portfolio Optimization

Portfolio Optimization involves the use of AI to maximize returns while minimizing risk according to a given risk tolerance:

- **Robo-Advisors**: These AI systems provide comprehensive portfolio management, including automatic rebalancing, asset allocation, and risk assessment.

- **Monte Carlo Simulation**: AI can run thousands of simulations to forecast potential outcomes under different market conditions, helping investors make more informed decisions.

- **Factor Investing Models**: AI models identify risk factors that influence asset prices and optimize portfolio exposure to these factors to maximize returns.

Machine Learning in Stock Selection

Using **Machine Learning** techniques, AI can analyze vast datasets to identify potential stock picks based on predicted price movements:

- **Supervised Learning**: AI models are trained on a set of features such as company fundamentals, price patterns, and economic indicators to predict stock performance.

- **Unsupervised Learning**: AI algorithms identify clusters or patterns within data without prior labeling, discovering new correlations that aren't readily apparent to human analysts.

- **Reinforcement Learning**: AI systems learn by continuously interacting with the market, making decisions based on rewards (profit) and penalties (loss).

Quantitative Investment Models

Quantitative Investment Models use mathematical computations to understand behavior and make predictions about financial markets and securities:

- **Factor Models**: AI analyzes various macroeconomic and microeconomic factors that might affect asset prices and incorporates them into stock valuation models.

- **Risk Models**: Advanced AI techniques assess and predict various types of risk, including market, credit, and operational risks, allowing investors to better manage their portfolios.

Implementing Advanced AI Techniques

- **Skill Development**: Investors should acquire a solid foundation in data science and machine learning or partner with AI experts.

- **Technology Investment**: Advanced AI investing requires access to powerful computing resources and high-quality data.
- **Ethical and Regulatory Compliance**: Ensure that AI applications comply with all relevant laws and ethical standards, particularly concerning data privacy and financial regulations.

Algorithmic Trading

Algorithmic trading, often known as "algo-trading," involves the use of computer algorithms to execute trading orders with speed and efficiency that human traders cannot match. This approach can significantly enhance trading strategies by automating complex, quantitative trading decisions based on predefined criteria.

Overview of Algorithmic Trading

Algorithmic trading utilizes mathematical models and algorithms to make trading decisions at high speeds and volumes, often executing orders within fractions of a second. These algorithms are designed to identify trading opportunities based on market data analysis and can operate without direct human intervention.

Types of Algorithmic Trading

1. **High-Frequency Trading (HFT)**: This type involves algorithms that trade stocks extremely quickly, often holding positions for just seconds or milliseconds. HFT strategies can exploit very small price discrepancies and market inefficiencies.
2. **Statistical Arbitrage**: Algorithms are used in this strategy to take advantage of pricing inefficiencies between securities. Statistical models are developed to identify profitable trading

opportunities from historical price relationships and market behaviors.

3. **Market Making**: In this strategy, algorithms are used to buy and sell securities, providing liquidity to the market. Market makers earn profits on the bid-ask spread while maintaining a balanced book of buys and sells.

4. **Sentiment Analysis**: Algorithms analyze market sentiment data from news sources, social media, and other text inputs to gauge market mood and predict potential price movements.

Advantages of Algorithmic Trading

- **Speed**: Algorithms can process vast amounts of data and execute trades at speeds impossible for humans, capturing opportunities that disappear in seconds.

- **Accuracy**: Automated trading minimizes human errors, executing trades precisely at desired price levels and quantities.

- **Discipline**: Trading is conducted strictly based on the algorithm's rules, reducing the risk of emotional trading decisions.

- **Cost-Efficiency**: By automating the trading process, algorithmic trading reduces the need for human traders, lowering operational costs.

Setting Up Algorithmic Trading

1. **Define Strategy**: Identify and define the trading strategy that the algorithm will implement. This involves selecting the trading criteria, indicators, and thresholds for entering and exiting trades.

2. **Backtesting**: Before going live, it's crucial to backtest the algorithm using historical data. This process helps verify the effectiveness of the trading strategy over different market conditions.

3. **Implementation**: Deploy the algorithm on a trading platform. Ensure robust connectivity and the ability to execute trades quickly and reliably.

4. **Monitoring**: Continuously monitor the algorithm's performance and make adjustments as needed. Monitoring is crucial to address any anomalies or technical issues that may arise.

Challenges and Considerations

- **Market Impact**: Large volume trades by algorithms can significantly impact market prices, especially in less liquid markets.

- **Regulatory Scrutiny**: Algorithmic trading is heavily scrutinized by regulators to prevent market manipulation and ensure fairness.

- **Technical Failures**: Reliance on technology means that glitches or system failures can result in unintended trades or loss of control over the trading process.

- **Complexity**: Developing and maintaining trading algorithms requires a deep understanding of both market dynamics and advanced programming skills.

Machine Learning Models for Predicting Stock Performance

Machine learning (ML) has become a crucial tool in the financial sector, enabling investors to predict stock performance with greater accuracy than traditional methods. These models can analyze large volumes of data, learn from historical trends, and identify patterns that may indicate future stock movements. This section explores how machine learning models are used to forecast stock performance and the types of models commonly employed.

Understanding Machine Learning in Finance

Machine learning in finance uses algorithms to process data, make predictions, and automatically improve through experience without being explicitly programmed. In stock market investing, ML models analyze historical data such as stock prices, trading volumes, financial statements, and even macroeconomic indicators to forecast future stock performance.

Types of Machine Learning Models Used in Stock Prediction

1. **Supervised Learning Models**: These models are trained on labeled data (data with predefined tags or labels showing past outcomes). They learn to predict the label for new data based on patterns recognized during training. Common supervised learning models include:
    - **Linear Regression**: Used for predicting a continuous value, such as the future price of a stock.
    - **Classification Models**: Such as logistic regression or support vector machines, used for predicting

categorical outcomes like whether a stock will go up or down.

2. **Time Series Forecasting**: This involves models that predict future values based on previously observed values. Time series models are especially suited for stock price predictions because they can account for trends, cycles, and seasonality. Examples include:
    - **ARIMA (AutoRegressive Integrated Moving Average)**: A model used for forecasting time series data.
    - **LSTM (Long Short-Term Memory networks)**: A type of recurrent neural network (RNN) that is particularly effective for sequences and series.

3. **Unsupervised Learning Models**: These models are used to identify patterns in data without pre-existing labels. They are often used to find hidden patterns or groupings in stock market data. Examples include:
    - **Clustering Algorithms**: Such as K-means for identifying groups of stocks that exhibit similar behavior.
    - **Principal Component Analysis (PCA)**: Used to reduce the dimensionality of financial datasets while preserving the most critical information.

4. **Reinforcement Learning**: In this model, algorithms learn to make sequences of decisions by receiving rewards or penalties. This type of learning can be used for dynamic investment strategies and portfolio management.
    - **Q-Learning**: An algorithm that learns the value of an action in a particular state and is used for making decisions under uncertain conditions.

Implementing Machine Learning Models

1. **Data Collection**: Gather historical data from various sources. This data might include historical stock prices, company financial statements, industry data, and macroeconomic indicators.

2. **Feature Engineering**: Transform raw data into features that better represent the problem to the predictive models, increasing their accuracy and effectiveness.

3. **Model Selection**: Choose appropriate machine learning models based on the nature of the data and the specific prediction task.

4. **Training and Testing**: Train the models on a designated training dataset and validate their performance using a separate testing set to avoid overfitting.

5. **Evaluation**: Use metrics such as accuracy, precision, recall, and F1 score for classification tasks, or mean squared error for regression tasks to evaluate the models.

6. **Deployment**: Implement the model in a real-time trading environment where it can provide ongoing predictions and insights.

Challenges and Considerations

- **Market Efficiency**: The stock market is highly efficient, meaning that all known information is already reflected in stock prices, which can limit the effectiveness of predictive models.

- **Data Quality**: Poor data quality can lead to inaccurate predictions. Ensuring data is clean, complete, and relevant is crucial.

- **Model Overfitting**: There is a risk that a model might perform well on historical data but poorly on unseen data. Regular updates and validations are necessary.

Advanced AI Tools for Risk Assessment

Risk assessment is a critical component of effective investment management. With the advent of advanced artificial intelligence (AI) technologies, investors can now utilize more sophisticated tools to analyze and mitigate risks associated with their investment portfolios. These AI tools enhance traditional risk management techniques by offering deeper insights, predictive capabilities, and real-time analysis. Here's how advanced AI tools are reshaping risk assessment in the investment world:

Types of Risks Addressed by AI Tools

1. **Market Risk**: The risk of losses due to factors that affect the entire market or asset class.
2. **Credit Risk**: The risk that a borrower will default on any type of debt.
3. **Liquidity Risk**: The risk arising from the difficulty of selling assets quickly at a fair price.
4. **Operational Risk**: Risks stemming from operational failures such as business disruptions, errors, or frauds.

Key AI Tools for Risk Assessment

- **Quantitative Risk Management Systems**: These systems use statistical and mathematical models to forecast potential losses in various risk scenarios. They can model the financial impact of risk factors such as market shifts, interest rate changes, or credit defaults.

- **Machine Learning Models**: Machine learning algorithms can predict defaults and potential price changes by analyzing patterns in large datasets, which include market data, economic indicators, and historical transaction records.

- **Natural Language Processing (NLP)**: NLP tools analyze unstructured data such as news articles, financial reports, and social media to gauge market sentiment and identify potential risk factors early. For instance, increasing negative sentiment or discussions around a specific sector might indicate an upcoming downturn.

- **Neural Networks**: Especially useful in detecting complex nonlinear patterns that traditional risk assessment models might miss. They are particularly effective in areas like fraud detection and anomaly detection, where patterns may be too subtle for less sophisticated algorithms.

- **Stress Testing and Scenario Analysis**: AI-enhanced stress testing tools simulate a variety of adverse economic scenarios to see how investments would perform under stress. These tools can adjust these scenarios in real-time as new data becomes available, providing ongoing insights into potential vulnerabilities.

Implementing AI in Risk Assessment

1. **Integration with Existing Systems**: AI tools should be integrated with existing risk management systems to enhance their capabilities. This integration allows for a more holistic view of risk across different levels of the organization.

2. **Data Quality and Management**: High-quality, relevant data is crucial for AI tools to function effectively. Ensuring accurate, clean, and comprehensive data feeds will improve the reliability of AI-driven risk assessments.

3. **Continuous Monitoring and Updating**: Risk factors and market conditions change rapidly. AI systems should be continually monitored and updated to ensure they adapt to new risks and incorporate the latest data.

4. **Expert Oversight**: While AI can provide significant insights and automate many aspects of risk assessment, human oversight remains crucial. Experts should interpret AI findings, considering contextual factors that the AI may not fully understand.

Challenges and Considerations

- **Model Bias and Transparency**: AI models can inherit biases from historical data, potentially leading to skewed risk assessments. Additionally, the "black box" nature of some AI models can make it difficult to understand how decisions are made, which is a significant consideration for regulatory compliance and ethical governance.

- **Regulatory Compliance**: As financial regulators increasingly focus on AI and machine learning, ensuring that AI tools comply with existing and forthcoming regulations is crucial.

09
THE FUTURE OF INVESTING WITH AI

Artificial Intelligence (AI) has already made significant inroads into the world of investing, transforming how decisions are made and potentially increasing the efficiency and accuracy of investments. As technology continues to advance, the role of AI in investing is expected to grow even more pronounced. This chapter explores the potential future developments in AI investing and how investors can prepare for these changes.

Trends and Developments in AI Investing

1. **Increased Automation**: Future investment platforms are likely to feature even greater levels of automation, with AI handling more complex decision-making tasks. This could lead to fully automated hedge funds and other investment funds that operate with minimal human oversight.

2. **Personalization at Scale**: AI will enable highly personalized investment services at a scale not previously possible. Algorithms will be able to create customized portfolios based on an individual's entire financial picture, including personal data, spending habits, and long-term financial goals.

3. **Integration of Alternative Data**: The use of unconventional data sources—such as satellite images, social media sentiment,

and internet traffic data—will become more mainstream. AI's ability to process and analyze this vast array of data will uncover new investment opportunities and insights.

4. **Advancements in Predictive Analytics**: AI models will become even more sophisticated, providing better forecasts and predictive insights for market movements. Enhanced machine learning models will be able to adapt more quickly to changing market conditions, offering real-time adjustments to investment strategies.

5. **Blockchain and AI Convergence**: The integration of AI with blockchain technology could revolutionize market security and transparency. AI could be used to manage and optimize blockchain operations, while blockchain could provide secure, tamper-proof data for AI algorithms.

Preparing for the Future

1. **Continuous Learning and Adaptation**: The field of AI is evolving rapidly. Investors should commit to continuous learning to keep up with new technologies and methods in AI investing. This includes staying informed through courses, seminars, and industry publications.

2. **Ethical and Responsible Investing**: As AI takes on more decision-making roles, issues of ethics and responsibility come to the forefront. Investors will need to consider the ethical implications of their AI strategies, including the impact on markets, the economy, and society.

3. **Collaboration between Humans and Machines**: The future of investing with AI will not be about replacing human investors but enhancing their capabilities. Successful strategies will likely

involve a collaborative approach where human intuition and expertise are augmented by AI's analytical power.

4. **Regulatory Compliance**: Investors must anticipate and adapt to regulatory changes as governments and financial bodies update rules to cope with the advancements in AI. Staying ahead of regulatory requirements and engaging with policymakers can help shape a favorable regulatory environment.

Challenges and Opportunities

- **Security and Privacy**: As AI systems handle more data and make more decisions, ensuring the security and privacy of data becomes crucial. Investors will need to invest in robust cybersecurity measures to protect both their assets and their clients' information.

- **Market Adaptation**: Markets themselves may change in response to widespread AI adoption. New forms of trading and investing may emerge, and traditional models may be disrupted.

- **Access and Inequality**: There is a risk that the benefits of AI in investing could be concentrated among those who can afford the latest technologies, potentially widening the gap between large institutional investors and individual retail investors. Addressing these disparities will be important for maintaining market fairness and accessibility.

Emerging Trends in AI and Investing

The rapid evolution of Artificial Intelligence (AI) technologies continues to reshape the landscape of investing. As AI tools become more sophisticated and prevalent, they are introducing new trends and opportunities in the financial sector. Understanding these emerging trends can help investors stay ahead of the curve and leverage AI effectively in their investment strategies. Here are some key trends to watch:

1. Democratization of Quantitative Investing

Traditionally, quantitative investing was primarily accessible to hedge funds and institutional investors due to the complexity and cost of the necessary technology and data. However, AI is democratizing access to these sophisticated strategies. With cloud computing and open-source AI platforms becoming more available, individual investors can now use quantitative tools and algorithms to enhance their investment decisions. This trend is lowering the barrier to entry and allowing more investors to leverage advanced analytical techniques.

2. AI-Driven Personalized Investing

AI technologies are making it possible to offer highly personalized investment services on a scale never before achievable. By analyzing individual financial data, spending habits, and personal goals, AI can tailor investment strategies uniquely suited to each investor's needs. This personalization extends beyond mere risk assessment to include lifestyle integration, where investment recommendations align closely with personal timelines and life goals.

3. Integration of Alternative Data

The use of alternative data in investment decision-making is growing. AI excels at processing and extracting insights from diverse data sources, including social media sentiments, geopolitical events, environmental data, and even satellite imagery. Investors are increasingly relying on AI to parse through this data to glean actionable insights that are not available through traditional financial metrics.

4. Real-Time Risk Management

AI's ability to analyze large volumes of data in real-time is revolutionizing risk management. Machine learning models can identify potential risks and anomalies as they occur, allowing investors to react instantly. This capability is critical in a global market where conditions change rapidly, and the speed of response can mean the difference between profit and loss.

5. Blockchain and AI Integration

Blockchain technology offers a secure, immutable ledger for transactions. When combined with AI, blockchain has the potential to further enhance the security and efficiency of investment processes. AI can optimize blockchain operations by automating smart contracts, performing predictive market analyses, and ensuring compliance through secure, transparent record-keeping.

6. AI Ethics and Regulation

As AI becomes more integral to investing, ethical considerations and regulatory compliance are gaining prominence. Investors and regulators alike are increasingly focused on issues such as data privacy, algorithmic bias, and the overall transparency of AI decision-making processes. This trend is leading to the development of new guidelines and frameworks to ensure that AI is used responsibly in the investment sector.

7. Advanced Simulation and Scenario Analysis

AI-powered simulation tools are becoming more sophisticated, allowing investors to model complex investment scenarios and stress tests with high accuracy. These simulations can account for a multitude of economic variables and potential market disruptions, providing investors with a detailed risk assessment and helping them prepare for different market conditions.

How to Stay Updated with AI Investment Technologies

As the field of AI continues to evolve rapidly, staying informed about the latest developments in AI investment technologies is crucial for investors who wish to maintain a competitive edge. Here are several effective strategies to help you keep abreast of the latest in AI-driven investment innovations:

1. Subscribe to Industry Publications

Dedicate time to read journals, magazines, and online publications that focus on AI, finance, and technology. Publications like *The Wall Street Journal*, *Financial Times*, and specialized outlets such as *AI in Finance* or *FinTech Futures* provide insights into current trends and new technologies in the finance sector.

2. Follow Thought Leaders and Influencers

Identify and follow thought leaders, industry experts, and influencers in AI and investing on social media platforms like LinkedIn, Twitter, and YouTube. These professionals often share valuable insights, discuss new tools, and provide analysis of recent advancements in AI technologies.

3. Participate in Webinars and Online Courses

Enroll in webinars and online courses that focus on the latest AI applications in finance. Many universities and private organizations offer courses on AI, machine learning, and their applications in investing that can help deepen your understanding and keep you updated.

4. Attend Conferences and Seminars

Attend industry conferences, seminars, and workshops that focus on AI and investing. Events such as the AI in Finance Summit, Finovate series, or local fintech meetups provide opportunities to hear from experts, participate in discussions, and network with peers who are also interested in the intersection of AI and finance.

5. Engage with Online Communities

Join online forums and communities where enthusiasts discuss AI and investing. Platforms like Reddit, Stack Exchange, or specialized online groups can be valuable resources for advice, discussions, and sharing knowledge about AI investment strategies and tools.

6. Utilize Professional Development Resources

If you're part of a professional organization, take advantage of the resources they offer. Many professional financial organizations provide members with access to training programs, literature, and the latest research on AI and other investment technologies.

7. Collaborate with Tech Providers

Establish relationships with technology providers and AI solution companies. These partnerships can provide access to cutting-edge tools, beta testing opportunities, and insights into how AI is being deployed in the investment sector.

8. Continuous Experimentation

Implement what you learn through small-scale experiments using AI tools and platforms. Practical application of AI technologies in your investing practices can provide firsthand experience with their capabilities and limitations, helping you stay at the forefront of technological advancements.

9. Monitor Regulatory Developments

Keep an eye on how regulatory frameworks around AI and investments are evolving. Changes in regulations can significantly affect how AI technologies are used in investing, and staying compliant is crucial.

Preparing for the Future of the Stock Market

The stock market is undergoing significant transformations due to advancements in technology, changes in global economic policies, and evolving investor behaviors. As an investor, preparing for the future of the stock market involves understanding these changes and adapting your strategies accordingly. Here are essential strategies to equip you for what lies ahead:

1. Embrace Technological Innovation

Technological advancements, particularly in AI and machine learning, are reshaping how investments are managed and decisions are made. To prepare:

- **Stay Informed**: Regularly update your knowledge about new technologies that impact investing, such as blockchain, AI, and big data analytics.

- **Adopt Technology**: Integrate advanced technologies into your investment processes, from automated trading systems to AI-driven risk assessment tools.

2. Understand and Adapt to Market Dynamics

The global economy is interconnected more than ever, making financial markets susceptible to international events and economic shifts. To adapt:

- **Global Awareness**: Stay informed about global economic conditions, including emerging markets, international trade policies, and geopolitical events that could affect the markets.

- **Flexibility in Strategies**: Be ready to adjust your investment strategies based on global economic trends. Diversify your investments to manage risks associated with economic uncertainties.

3. Develop a Long-Term Perspective

While short-term market fluctuations can provide opportunities for quick gains, a long-term perspective can help in building sustainable wealth. To develop this perspective:

- **Focus on Long-Term Goals**: Align your investment choices with long-term financial goals, such as retirement planning or wealth transfer.

- **Resist Overreaction**: Avoid making impulsive decisions based on short-term market volatility. Focus on steady growth over time.

4. Foster Financial Literacy

Continuing to educate yourself about financial markets and investment strategies is crucial. To improve your financial literacy:

- **Continuous Learning**: Engage in ongoing education through courses, webinars, and seminars. Focus on both the fundamentals of investing and advanced topics like quantitative finance.

- **Utilize Expert Advice**: Consult with financial advisors and use credible financial analysis services to enhance your understanding and decision-making.

5. Monitor Regulatory Changes

Regulations in the financial markets are constantly evolving to adapt to new technologies and economic realities. To stay ahead:

- **Stay Updated**: Keep abreast of changes in securities law, taxation, and corporate governance that could impact your investments.

- **Compliance**: Ensure that your investment activities always remain compliant with the latest regulations to avoid legal complications.

6. Prepare for Increased Volatility

Market volatility is expected to continue, driven by rapid technological changes, economic policies, and other factors. To manage this volatility:

- **Risk Management**: Employ advanced risk management strategies, such as using stop-loss orders and hedging.

- **Maintain Liquidity**: Ensure you have sufficient liquidity to manage and exploit the opportunities presented by market volatility.

7. Cultivate a Diverse Investment Portfolio

Diversification remains a key strategy for preparing for future market uncertainties. To effectively diversify:

- **Explore Various Asset Classes**: Invest in a mix of stocks, bonds, real estate, and alternative investments like cryptocurrencies or commodities.

- **Geographic Diversification**: Consider investments in international markets to spread risk across different economic environments.

10

BUILDING A LONG-TERM INVESTMENT PLAN

Investing with a long-term perspective is essential for achieving substantial growth and meeting significant financial goals such as retirement, buying a home, or funding education. This chapter outlines strategies to construct a robust long-term investment plan that utilizes both traditional approaches and modern AI tools to optimize your portfolio's performance over time.

Define Your Financial Goals

Start by clearly defining your long-term financial objectives. Consider what you aim to achieve with your investments:

- **Retirement Savings**: Determine how much you will need to live comfortably in retirement.

- **Wealth Accumulation**: Set targets for wealth creation that may include buying property or growing your personal wealth for future generations.

- **Major Expenditures**: Plan for significant future expenses like children's education or a dream vacation.

Assess Your Time Horizon and Risk Tolerance

Understanding your investment horizon and how much risk you can tolerate is crucial in shaping your investment strategy:

- **Time Horizon**: Your age and the time frame for each financial goal will influence your investment strategy. Longer horizons usually allow for taking on more risk.

- **Risk Tolerance**: Assess your comfort with risk. Younger investors may opt for a more aggressive portfolio, while those nearing retirement may prefer conservative investments.

Develop a Diversified Asset Allocation

Diversification across different asset classes can reduce risk and stabilize returns over the long term:

- **Asset Allocation**: Spread your investments across stocks, bonds, real estate, and other assets. The allocation should reflect your risk tolerance and time horizon.

- **Rebalancing**: Regularly adjust your portfolio to maintain your desired asset allocation. AI tools can automate this process, ensuring your portfolio stays aligned with your goals.

Utilize AI for Enhanced Portfolio Management

Incorporate AI tools to improve decision-making and maintain a competitive edge:

- **Robo-Advisors**: Use robo-advisors for automated portfolio management, which can include selecting investments, rebalancing, and tax optimization.

- **Predictive Analytics**: Leverage AI-driven predictive analytics to identify potential high-growth opportunities and avoid possible downturns.

Implement Strategic Tax Planning

Efficient tax planning can significantly affect your investment returns and should be an integral part of your long-term investment strategy:

- **Tax-Efficient Investing**: Consider tax-advantaged accounts like IRAs and 401(k)s. Use strategies like tax-loss harvesting to offset gains with losses.

- **Regular Reviews**: Regularly review your tax strategies to adapt to changes in tax laws and your financial situation.

Monitor and Adjust the Plan Regularly

An effective long-term investment plan requires ongoing attention and adjustment:

- **Performance Monitoring**: Use AI tools and dashboards to monitor your portfolio's performance regularly.

- **Life Changes**: Update your investment plan in response to major life events such as marriage, the birth of a child, or career changes.

- **Market Conditions**: Adjust your strategies based on changing economic and market conditions. Stay informed about global economic trends and their potential impact on investments.

Stay Educated and Seek Professional Advice

Continuously educate yourself about financial markets and investment strategies. Additionally, consult with financial advisors to gain professional insights and guidance:

- **Continuous Learning**: Engage in lifelong learning through courses, seminars, and financial literature.

- **Professional Advice**: Even with advanced AI tools at your disposal, the value of professional human judgment and experience cannot be underestimated.

Long-Term Investment Strategies

Investing with a long-term perspective is crucial for achieving substantial financial growth and securing your financial future. This approach involves more than merely holding investments over an extended period; it requires a strategic plan that incorporates diversified asset allocation, regular portfolio reviews, and adjustments based on changing economic and personal circumstances. Here are essential strategies to enhance your long-term investment success:

Focus on Diversification

Diversification is a foundational strategy for long-term investment success. It involves spreading your investments across various asset classes, sectors, geographic locations, and investment styles to mitigate risk and reduce the impact of volatility on your portfolio. Effective diversification strategies include:

- **Asset Class Diversification**: Invest in a mix of stocks, bonds, real estate, and potentially alternative investments like commodities or private equity.

- **Geographical Diversification**: Allocate investments across global markets to take advantage of economic growth in different regions and hedge against local economic downturns.

- **Sector Diversification**: Spread investments across different sectors to reduce sector-specific risks and capitalize on growth in various industries.

Embrace a Buy-and-Hold Philosophy

The buy-and-hold strategy involves purchasing securities and holding them over a long period, regardless of fluctuations in the market. This strategy benefits from:

- **Compounding Returns**: Allowing earnings to generate their own earnings over time.
- **Reduced Transaction Costs**: Minimizing costs associated with frequent trading, such as commissions and taxes.
- **Market Timing Avoidance**: Eliminating the risk of poor timing decisions that can lead to significant losses.

Regular Rebalancing

To maintain the intended risk level and return potential of your portfolio, regular rebalancing is essential. This involves:

- **Periodic Reviews**: Assessing the portfolio at regular intervals (e.g., annually or semi-annually) to determine if the asset allocation still aligns with your investment goals and risk tolerance.
- **Adjusting Proportions**: Buying or selling assets to return to your original asset allocation, taking advantage of systematic buying low and selling high.

Utilize Tax-Efficient Investing Strategies

Tax efficiency is crucial in maximizing returns over the long term. Strategies to enhance tax efficiency include:

- **Tax-Advantaged Accounts**: Making use of IRAs, 401(k)s, and other retirement accounts that offer tax benefits either at the time of deposit or upon withdrawal.

- **Tax-Loss Harvesting**: Selling securities at a loss to offset a capital gains tax liability.
- **Holding Periods**: Holding assets for over a year to benefit from lower long-term capital gains tax rates.

Leverage Technology and AI

Incorporate advanced technologies and AI tools to enhance decision-making and improve portfolio performance:

- **Robo-Advisors**: Utilizing AI-driven advisors for automated portfolio management, including rebalancing and tax optimization.
- **AI Analysis Tools**: Employing advanced analytics for predictive insights and deeper understanding of market trends and investment opportunities.

Stay Informed and Flexible

The economic landscape and your personal circumstances will evolve, requiring a flexible approach to your investment strategy:

- **Continuous Education**: Keeping abreast of economic, political, and financial developments that might impact your investments.
- **Professional Advice**: Consulting with financial advisors for expert insights and personalized advice tailored to your financial situation.

Incorporating AI into Long-Term Planning

The integration of Artificial Intelligence (AI) into long-term investment strategies offers a unique opportunity to enhance decision-making, optimize portfolio performance, and adapt to changing market conditions more dynamically. Here's how AI can be effectively incorporated into long-term financial planning:

AI-Driven Portfolio Management

Automated Asset Allocation and Rebalancing: AI-driven tools, such as robo-advisors, can automate the process of asset allocation based on predefined goals and risk tolerance. These tools continuously monitor the market and the portfolio, making adjustments and rebalancing assets to maintain target allocations, which is crucial for long-term investment strategies.

Tax Optimization: AI can help in identifying opportunities for tax-loss harvesting and other strategies to minimize tax liabilities over time. This is particularly valuable for long-term investors looking to maximize their after-tax returns.

Predictive Analytics for Strategic Planning

Market Trend Analysis: Machine learning models can analyze historical data and identify underlying trends and patterns. Investors can use these insights to anticipate market movements and adjust their strategies accordingly.

Risk Assessment: Advanced AI models can predict potential risks by analyzing a variety of factors, including market volatility, economic indicators, and geopolitical events. This allows investors to proactively manage risks before they impact the portfolio significantly.

Enhanced Decision Support

Scenario Analysis and Stress Testing: AI can simulate various economic and market scenarios to see how different strategies might perform under various conditions. This is invaluable for long-term planning, as it helps investors prepare for different potential futures.

Real-Time Data Processing: AI's ability to process and analyze data in real-time ensures that long-term investment decisions are based on the most current information, helping to align strategies with the latest market conditions.

Personalized Investment Strategies

Tailored Recommendations: AI can process personal financial data, including income, expenses, life goals, and more, to provide highly personalized investment advice. This customization is key in long-term planning, ensuring that strategies are uniquely aligned with individual financial goals.

Behavioral Finance Insights: AI tools can analyze an investor's behavior and decision-making patterns, offering insights that can help mitigate biases and improve financial decisions. This is particularly useful in long-term planning, where emotional investing can derail financial goals.

Continuous Learning and Adaptation

Machine Learning Improvements: AI systems are designed to learn and improve from new data continuously. In a long-term investment context, this means that AI tools can adapt and evolve with the financial markets, enhancing their predictive accuracy and utility over time.

Feedback Loops: Incorporating feedback mechanisms can help refine AI systems, ensuring that they remain aligned with the investor's goals and adapt to changing preferences and circumstances.

Implementation Considerations

Integration with Existing Systems: Ensure that AI tools seamlessly integrate with existing financial planning systems and workflows to enhance rather than disrupt processes.

Security and Privacy: Given the sensitive nature of financial data, security and privacy considerations are paramount when incorporating AI into long-term planning.

Regulatory Compliance: Stay informed about and compliant with regulations governing the use of AI in financial services, particularly those relating to data usage and consumer rights.

Sustaining Growth: AI and Continuous Learning

In the rapidly evolving world of finance, sustaining growth increasingly relies on leveraging advanced technologies like Artificial Intelligence (AI). AI's capability for continuous learning — the ability to constantly adapt and improve from new data — makes it an invaluable tool for investors seeking to maintain and enhance their financial growth over time. Here's how AI and continuous learning can be pivotal in sustaining long-term investment growth:

Leveraging AI for Dynamic Market Adaptation

Real-Time Data Analysis: AI systems are designed to handle and analyze vast amounts of data in real time. For investors, this means being able to quickly adjust to market changes and capitalize on opportunities as they arise, ensuring that investment strategies remain relevant and effective.

Predictive Analytics: AI's predictive capabilities are rooted in its ability to learn and adapt from historical and current data. This allows for more accurate forecasting of market trends and asset performance, providing investors with a proactive approach to managing investments and mitigating risks.

Enhancing Decision-Making with Machine Learning

Pattern Recognition: Machine learning algorithms excel at identifying complex patterns in data that human analysts might overlook. This capability can lead to better decision-making by revealing hidden insights in market movements, consumer behavior, and economic indicators.

Scenario Analysis and Simulation: AI can simulate various investment scenarios based on historical data and hypothetical situations. This continuous learning process allows investors to test different strategies and prepare for potential future conditions without real-world risk.

Personalizing Investment Strategies

Customization at Scale: AI provides personalized investment advice and management by learning individual preferences, risk tolerances, and financial goals. Over time, as it gathers more data, AI can refine and adjust its recommendations to better align with the investor's evolving needs.

Behavioral Analytics: AI tools also incorporate behavioral analytics to understand investor behaviors and biases. By continuously learning from investor actions, AI can help in crafting strategies that not only meet financial goals but also align with the investor's investment style and behavior.

Continuous Improvement and Adaptation

Feedback Mechanisms: One of the key aspects of AI in investing is its ability to incorporate feedback to improve its algorithms. Continuous learning from successes and failures makes AI progressively smarter, enhancing its effectiveness as a financial tool.

Integration with New Technologies: As new technologies and data sources emerge, AI systems can integrate these into their operations, continually enhancing their capabilities and providing investors with cutting-edge tools.

Overcoming Challenges with AI Continuous Learning

Data Quality and Privacy: Continuous learning requires access to high-quality, large datasets. Ensuring data integrity and security, especially personal and sensitive information, is crucial.

Regulatory Compliance: As AI becomes more autonomous, staying compliant with evolving financial regulations is necessary to ensure ethical and legal use of AI in investing.

Human Oversight: Despite AI's capabilities, human oversight remains crucial. Continuous collaboration between AI systems and human judgment ensures that AI supports rather than replaces human expertise.

GLOSSARY OF INVESTMENT AND AI TERMS

Algorithmic Trading: The use of computer algorithms to automatically make trading decisions, execute trades, and manage portfolios.

Asset Allocation: The strategy of distributing investments among various financial categories like stocks, bonds, and cash to optimize risk and reward based on an individual's goals, risk tolerance, and investment horizon.

Behavioral Analytics: The technology used to study consumer behavior using data collected from digital interactions, aiming to improve business outcomes and predict future behaviors.

Blockchain: A decentralized digital ledger that records transactions across many computers so that the record cannot be altered retroactively without the alteration of all subsequent blocks.

Bull Market: A financial market of a group of securities in which prices are rising or are expected to rise.

Bear Market: A market condition in which the prices of securities are falling, and widespread pessimism causes the negative sentiment to be self-sustaining.

Classification Models: In machine learning, these models predict discrete responses, identifying which category an outcome belongs to (e.g., whether a stock price will go up or down).

Data Mining: The practice of examining large databases to generate new information and find hidden patterns.

Diversification: An investment strategy that aims to reduce risk by allocating investments among various financial instruments, industries, and other categories.

ETF (Exchange-Traded Fund): Investment funds traded on stock exchanges, much like stocks, that hold assets such as stocks, commodities, or bonds and generally operate with an arbitrage mechanism.

Financial Modeling: The process of creating a summary of a company's expenses and earnings in the form of a spreadsheet that can be used to calculate the impact of a future event or decision.

High-Frequency Trading (HFT): A type of algorithmic trading characterized by high speeds, high turnover rates, and high order-to-trade ratios that leverages high-frequency financial data and electronic trading tools.

Machine Learning: A subset of AI that enables systems to learn from data, identify patterns, and make decisions with minimal human intervention.

Market Sentiment: The overall attitude of investors toward a particular security or financial market.

Natural Language Processing (NLP): A branch of AI that helps computers understand, interpret, and produce human language.

Neural Networks: A series of algorithms that attempt to recognize underlying relationships in a set of data through a process that mimics the way the human brain operates.

Portfolio Management: The art and science of making decisions about investment mix and policy, matching investments to objectives, asset allocation for individuals and institutions, and balancing risk against performance.

Predictive Analytics: The use of data, statistical algorithms, and machine learning techniques to identify the likelihood of future outcomes based on historical data.

Quantitative Investing: An investment approach that employs quantitative techniques to analyze financial data and make investment decisions.

Rebalancing: The process of realigning the weightings of a portfolio of assets as investment prices change.

Risk Management: The process of identification, analysis, and acceptance or mitigation of uncertainty in investment decisions.

Robo-Advisor: A digital platform that provides automated, algorithm-driven financial planning services with little to no human supervision.

Time Series Analysis: A statistical technique that deals with time series data, or trend analysis, to forecast future events based on known past events.

Appendices

Appendix A: Case Studies of AI in Investing

Provide detailed case studies that highlight successful applications of AI in investing. Each case study should discuss the scenario, the AI technology used, implementation strategies, challenges faced, and the outcomes. This can help readers see real-world applications of concepts discussed in the book.

Appendix B: List of AI Investment Tools and Platforms

Include a comprehensive list of current AI tools and platforms available for investors, along with brief descriptions, features, and intended user types. This could also include links to websites or other resources for further investigation.

Appendix C: Step-by-Step Guides to Setting Up AI Tools

Offer practical, step-by-step instructions on how to set up and use some of the most popular AI investment tools. This can be a how-to guide for tools like robo-advisors, AI-driven analytics platforms, and algorithmic trading systems.

Appendix D: Investment Checklist

Provide a checklist that investors can use to evaluate AI investment tools and platforms, assess stock options using AI analytics, or prepare for making investment decisions using AI insights. This checklist can help ensure that readers perform due diligence before making investment decisions.

Appendix E: Glossary of Advanced AI and Financial Terms

A comprehensive glossary that goes beyond the basics to include more advanced terms used in AI and financial industries. This will be useful for readers who wish to delve deeper into more complex topics or need clarifications on advanced content.

Appendix F: Interviews with Industry Experts

Transcripts or summaries of interviews with AI technology developers, financial analysts, and experienced investors who use AI. These interviews can provide insights into the current trends, future outlook, and practical advice for new investors using AI.

Appendix G: Regulatory Considerations in AI Investing

A detailed guide on current regulations affecting AI in investing, including privacy laws, data usage, and ethical considerations. This can also include guidance on how to stay compliant while using AI tools in various jurisdictions.

Appendix H: Further Reading and Resources

A curated list of books, articles, journals, and online courses for readers who wish to further their understanding of AI in investing. This list should be categorized based on topics such as AI fundamentals, machine learning, financial analytics, etc.

Appendix I: FAQ on AI and Investing

A compilation of frequently asked questions about using AI in investing, with comprehensive answers that address common concerns and misconceptions. This can help clarify doubts and provide quick answers to the most common queries.

Appendix J: Sample Investment Strategies Using AI

Provide examples of various investment strategies enhanced by AI, including conservative, balanced, and aggressive portfolios. Explain how AI influences the asset allocation and management of each strategy.

Appendix A: How to Access and Use Investment Platforms

Navigating the world of investment platforms can be daunting for beginners. This appendix provides a step-by-step guide on how to access and effectively use various investment platforms, particularly focusing on those that incorporate AI technologies.

1. Choosing the Right Investment Platform

Determine Your Needs: Assess your investment goals, risk tolerance, and desired level of involvement (active vs. passive investing).

Research Platforms: Look for platforms that match your investment style. Consider factors such as user interface, fees, available assets, AI integration, and educational resources.

Read Reviews and Ratings: Check out reviews from other users and professional ratings to gauge the reliability and performance of the platform.

2. Setting Up Your Investment Account

Registration Process: Typically involves providing personal information such as your name, address, social security number, employment information, and financial situation.

Identity Verification: You may need to submit identification documents to comply with regulatory requirements, known as "Know Your Customer" (KYC) procedures.

Funding Your Account: Link your bank account or arrange for a wire transfer to deposit funds into your investment account.

3. Navigating the Platform

Dashboard: Familiarize yourself with the platform's dashboard. This is your main interface, where you can view your account balance, performance statistics, and access trading tools.

Educational Resources: Utilize any tutorials, webinars, or articles provided by the platform to better understand how to use the platform and make informed investment decisions.

Customer Support: Know how to access support. Many platforms offer live chat, email support, and phone lines.

4. Making Your First Investment

Research Tools: Use the platform's research tools to analyze potential investments. AI-enhanced platforms may offer predictive analytics, risk assessments, and automated portfolio suggestions.

Placing Orders: Learn how to place trade orders. Most platforms will offer a variety of order types, such as market orders, limit orders, and stop-loss orders.

Monitoring Investments: Set up alerts or use the platform's monitoring tools to keep track of your investments' performance and market changes.

5. Using AI Features

Automated Portfolio Management: If using a robo-advisor, set your investment criteria based on your risk tolerance and goals. The AI will manage asset allocation and rebalancing.

AI Analytics Tools: Engage with tools that provide AI-driven market analysis, sentiment analysis, and predictive forecasting.

Customization and Feedback: Customize AI settings if possible, and provide feedback to improve AI recommendations, adapting to your investment style and preferences.

6. Regular Maintenance and Updates

Review and Rebalance: Regularly review your portfolio's performance through the platform. Rebalance manually or adjust settings for automatic rebalancing by AI.

Stay Updated: Keep your platform updated, and stay informed about new features or tools that can enhance your investment strategy.

Security Practices: Regularly update your passwords, and enable two-factor authentication (2FA) to secure your investment account.

Appendix B: Resources for Further Learning

To continue expanding your knowledge about investing and AI, here is a curated list of resources including books, online courses, websites, and podcasts that cater to a range of expertise levels, from beginners to advanced learners.

Books

1. **"The Intelligent Investor" by Benjamin Graham** - A seminal book in investment literature, offering foundational knowledge in value investing.

2. **"Flash Boys" by Michael Lewis** - Explores the impact of high-frequency trading on the financial markets.

3. **"Predictably Irrational" by Dan Ariely** - Provides insights into behavioral economics, crucial for understanding market psychology.

4. **"Machine Learning for Asset Managers" by Marcos Lopez de Prado** - Discusses modern machine learning approaches in asset management.

5. **"Artificial Intelligence in Finance: A Python-Based Guide" by Yves Hilpisch** - A practical guide to implementing AI algorithms in financial analysis.

Online Courses

1. **Coursera – AI For Everyone by Andrew Ng** - A non-technical course that explains the implications and applications of AI across various industries.

2. **Udemy – Python for Financial Analysis and Algorithmic Trading** - Teaches how to use Python for financial analysis and algorithmic trading.

3. **edX – Investment Management with Python and Machine Learning Specialization** - Offers a hands-on approach to investment management using Python and machine learning.

4. **MIT OpenCourseWare – Artificial Intelligence** - A free course providing a broad understanding of AI principles and techniques.

Websites

1. **Investopedia** - Offers a wealth of articles, tutorials, and simulators to help understand all aspects of investing.

2. **Seeking Alpha** - Provides stock market insights and financial analysis from a community of investors and industry experts.

3. **Kaggle** - Hosts AI and machine learning competitions where datasets related to financial markets are often featured.

4. **Quantopian** - A platform for building, testing, and executing trading algorithms.

Podcasts

1. **Chat With Traders** - Features successful traders who share their experiences and strategies.

2. **The AI Alignment Podcast** - Explores the research and technology behind AI safety and alignment through interviews with experts.

3. **Invest Like the Best** - Host Sean O'Shaughnessy talks with experts across the investment world to uncover new strategies and insights.

Professional Journals

1. **The Journal of Finance** - Publishes leading research across all the major fields of financial research.
2. **Journal of Financial Data Science** - Focuses on how data science is applied in financial markets.
3. **Machine Learning Research** - Provides open access to research on machine learning and computational models.

Index

A

- AI-Driven Market Analysis, 78
- AI Investment Tools, 51
- Algorithmic Trading, 43, 80, 81, 84
- Asset Allocation, 28, 70, 73, 105, Glossary
- Automated Trading, 79

B

- Behavioral Analytics, 113, 115, Glossary
- Blockchain Technology, 97
- Bull and Bear Markets

C

- Case Studies, 66, Appendix A
- Classification Models, 87, 115, Glossary
- Continuous Learning, 77, 102, 106

- Credit Risk, 90

D

- Data Mining, 115, Glossary
- Diversification, 24, 28, 70
- Dynamic Asset Allocation

E

- ETFs (Exchange-Traded Funds), 9, 17, Glossary
- Ethical Investing, 125
- Event-Driven Trading, 82, Glossary

F

- Financial Goals, 104
- Flash Trading, Glossary

G

- Glossary, 115

H

- High-Frequency Trading (HFT), 81, 84, Glossary

I

- Investment Platforms, 53, Appendix A
- Investment Strategies, 107

L

- Liquidity Risk, 21, 90
- Long-Term Investment Strategies, 107

M

- Market Risk, 20, 90
- Machine Learning, 41, 87, Glossary
- Monte Carlo Simulation, 82, Glossary

N

- Natural Language Processing (NLP), 41, 56, 91, 116, Glossary

O

- Operational Risk, 90

P

- Portfolio Management, 39, 53, 116
- Predictive Analytics, 39, 60, 62, 77, 78, 82, 105, 113
- Privacy in AI Investing

Q

- Quantitative Investing, 117, Glossary

R

- Real-Time Data Processing, 111
- Rebalancing, 70, 105, 117
- Regulatory Compliance, 92, 95, 112, 114

S

- Sentiment Analysis, 62, 65, 85, 82
- Statistical Arbitrage, 81, 84
- Stress Testing, 76

T

- Tax Efficiency, 12
- Time Series Analysis, 82, Glossary

U

- Unsupervised Learning, 83, 88 Glossary

V

- Volatility, 14, 76, 103

W

- Wealth Management,
- Webinars and Online Learning,

Z

- Zero-Sum Trading,

About the Author

Ernie Braveboy is a seasoned financial analyst with extensive experience in stock market investing and real estate. His diverse investment portfolio has allowed him to develop a deep understanding of different market dynamics and investment strategies, making him a respected authority in the financial sector.

Throughout his career, Ernie has actively managed multiple investments in both the stock market and real estate, giving him unique insights into asset allocation, risk management, and wealth optimization. His hands-on experience in these fields fuels his passion for teaching others, aiming to make sophisticated investment strategies accessible to all.

A regular contributor to major financial publications, Ernie also shares his expertise through speaking engagements at national and international finance conferences. His writings and talks often focus on how to utilize artificial intelligence to enhance investment decisions, a testimony to his belief in the power of technology to democratize finance.

In his book, "No Experience? No Problem! Investing in Stocks with AI Assistance," Ernie distills his years of investing experience into understandable strategies that leverage AI technology. He aims to bridge the gap between complex financial theories and practical, profitable investment practices.

Request for a Review

Dear Reader,

Thank you so much for purchasing and reading "No Experience? No Problem! Investing in Stocks with AI Assistance." I hope you found the insights and strategies shared within these pages both informative and applicable to your investment journey.

If you have a moment, I would greatly appreciate it if you could share your thoughts about the book by leaving a review on Amazon. Your feedback not only helps me to improve my work but also assists other potential readers in making an informed decision.

Leaving a review is simple:

1. Go to the product page on Amazon.
2. Scroll down to the "Customer Reviews" section.
3. Click on "Write a customer review."
4. Rate the book and write a few sentences about what you thought of it.

Every review counts, and your opinion is invaluable to both me and future readers. Thank you once again for your support and for taking the time to share your thoughts.

Warm regards,

Ernie Braveboy

Book Preview: AI Freelancing 101: Your First Step to Six Figures

Are you ready to harness the power of Artificial Intelligence and turn it into a lucrative freelancing career? "AI Freelancing 101: Your First Step to Six Figures" is your essential guide to navigating the rapidly growing field of AI freelancing. Whether you are new to the freelancing world or looking to pivot your career towards AI, this book provides the foundational knowledge you need to start, manage, and grow a profitable AI freelancing business.

What You Will Learn:

- **Understanding AI and Its Market Demand**: Grasp the basics of AI technologies and why they're in high demand across various industries. Learn how AI is transforming businesses and creating ample opportunities for skilled freelancers.

- **Identifying AI Skills in Demand**: Dive into the most sought-after AI skills in the freelance market. Whether it's machine learning, natural language processing, or data analysis, find out which skills you need to master to attract top-paying clients.

- **Building Your AI Skill Set**: Step-by-step instructions on how to acquire AI skills. The book provides resources for self-learning, including courses, certifications, and practical projects to build your portfolio.

- **Launching Your Freelance Business**: Get practical advice on setting up your freelancing business. From registering your business to setting up your digital presence and tools necessary to manage projects and clients effectively.

- **Marketing Your Services**: Learn how to market your AI skills effectively to stand out in a competitive market. Tips on crafting compelling proposals, optimizing your profile on freelancing platforms, and utilizing social media to attract clients.

- **Pricing Strategies**: Understand how to price your services to reflect your skills and expertise while remaining competitive. Learn negotiation tactics to ensure you're paid what you're worth.

- **Managing Projects and Client Relationships**: Best practices for managing projects efficiently and maintaining positive client relationships to ensure repeat business and steady income.

- **Scaling Your Business**: Strategies for scaling your freelancing business from a solo operation to a thriving enterprise. Learn how to hire and manage a team, expand your service offerings, and increase your earning potential.

Who Should Read This Book?

This book is designed for individuals who are intrigued by the potential of AI and are looking to leverage their technical skills in a freelance capacity. Whether you are a complete beginner in AI or have some technical background, this book will guide you through making AI freelancing a successful and profitable career choice.

Connect With Me on Social Media

Stay engaged and join our growing community on social media! Follow me for more updates, live discussions, and a behind-the-scenes look at my writing process. You can also share your thoughts, participate in community polls, and get exclusive content. Here's where you can find me:

- **TikTok**: Follow me on TikTok for quick tips and engaging video content at @erniebraveboy.
- **Facebook**: Join our community on Facebook for updates and interactions at Ernie Braveboy's Facebook Page.
- **Instagram**: Get a visual snapshot of my work and daily insights on Instagram @erniebraveboy.

I love connecting with readers and fellow enthusiasts, so don't hesitate to reach out and engage through these platforms. Your support and feedback are incredibly valuable to me.

www.ingramcontent.com/pod-product-compliance
Lightning Source LLC
Chambersburg PA
CBHW070249230526
45470CB00002B/535